ENI

"In *Now My Eyes See You,* Janell Kremer masterfully guides us through the transformative journey from pain to encounter, revealing the profound truth that God's presence is unwavering amidst our deepest struggles. Drawing from her own poignant experiences, Janell tenderly illustrates how moments of brokenness can serve as divine invitations to behold God's face, offering solace, healing, and, ultimately, victory in Jesus.

Through this 6-week devotional, Janell invites us to embrace our pain not as a burden but as a gateway to profound spiritual intimacy. With each page, she illuminates life-altering truths that resonate with Scripture's timeless wisdom, guiding readers toward a deeper understanding of God's boundless love and unfailing grace.

Now My Eyes See You is more than just a book; it's a beacon of hope for anyone navigating the turbulent waters of suffering. Janell's words are a testament to the resilience of the human spirit and the immeasurable depth of God's compassion. This devotional is a must-read for all who seek solace in adversity and long to encounter the living God face-to-face."

—Dr. Brian Simmons
Passion & Fire Ministries

"Do you yearn for a more intimate and meaningful relationship with God? Do you want to know Him more fully and see Him more clearly? If so, Janell Kremer's devotional book, *Now My Eyes See You,* is the perfect companion on your spiritual journey. This beautiful devotional offers a six-week spiritual encounter designed to deepen your understanding of God's presence in your life.

Janell's personal journey of experiencing God's profound love in the middle of a profound trial will encourage you and your faith. Her warm and relatable writing style will make you feel like you're having a heartfelt conversation with a close friend, all while guiding you closer to God. I'm excited for you to encounter the Lord through the pages of this book!"

—Dr. Patricia King
Author, Minister, Media Producer and Host

"What an *uplifting* and *inspiring* devotional for anyone walking through a season of pain, difficulty, or tragedy. As you journey through each daily devotional, you will be drawn to experience the love of the Father in a profound and life-changing way."

—Pam Johnson
Lead Care Pastor, River Valley Church

"So many of us struggle to process our suffering. Questions like, "Why?" "How?" and "Where was God in it all?" test our faith and trust in God's goodness. In her powerful devotional, *Now My Eyes See You,* Janell Kremer invites us on a profound exploration of faith in the face of pain. Through her own miraculous healing experience and insightful reflections from the book of Job, she guides readers on a six-week journey of transforming suffering into a catalyst for deeper faith. Whether you're facing a recent heartbreak, a chronic illness, or life's daily challenges, this book offers genuine hope.

With wisdom and grace, Janell reminds us that God doesn't waste our pain; He uses it to refine us and draw us closer to Himself. *Now My Eyes See You* is a tool for those seeking to connect more intimately with Jesus so that, like Job, life's painful experiences bring them face-to-face with the God of all comfort, peace, and true restoration.

—Teresa and Jeremiah Yancy
Founders, Unlocking Your Book
Authors, *The Messenger Life*

"In *Now My Eyes See You,* Janell Kremer gives powerful daily guidance for accepting God's invitations to taste His goodness in spite of and in the midst of—our painful trials and 'why me' questions. With the book of Job staging the puzzling dichotomies of our human experiences, Janell's devotions point to a faithful God who we can trust to care for us in the most intimate and unique ways. Learn to be keen to the schemes of the enemy while turning your focus on Jesus to go from 'coping to conquering.'"

—Tahni Cullen
Coauthor of *Josiah's Fire: Autism Stole His Words, God Gave Him a Voice*

"Nothing can separate us from the love of God, but suffering can make us question this reality. In this devotional, Janell writes with honesty and authenticity, helping readers discover a place of safety under the shadow of His wings. If you're ready to encounter God in deeper ways and take back ground that the enemy tried to steal in your life, this book is for you."

—Lauren Gaskill
Author, speaker, and founder of *She Found Joy*

"God is everything He says He is, but He is so much more impactful through the words and different ways He talks to us. Janell Kremer talks with God often and hears from Him. This devotional is God speaking to all of us through the words He has given her to write on these pages. She is a powerful woman of God. I can say with confidence that the Lord is pleased with this devotional as it brings truth to us and over us."

—Mark Bettenga
Care Pastor, River Valley Church

NOW MY EYES SEE

You

A SIX WEEK DEVOTIONAL

NOW MY EYES SEE You

WHEN PAIN BECOMES AN INVITATION TO ENCOUNTER GOD FACE-TO-FACE

JANELL KREMER

ISBN Paperback: 978-1-961557-50-5

ISBN Ebook: 978-1-961557-51-2

Library of Congress Control Number: 9781961557505

Messenger Books
30 N. Gould Ste. R
Sheridan, WY 82801

CONTENTS

To my two beautiful children, Ella and Calvin.

Watching you both grow in the Lord has been the most incredible privilege of my life. I am honored to be your mother and excited to see the love of Christ flow through you to reach those in pain. My prayer is that you will remain faithful to our faithful God. Listen to the Holy Spirit, no matter what He asks of you. When the darkness appears to be winning the battle, do not forget that God made you for such a time as this. God chose you both to carry His glory into every atmosphere you encounter, pointing others to the source of life. May you keep your eyes fixed on Jesus and your hearts pure, for He's coming back soon.

A SAFE PLACE FOR SUFFERING

"You have to jump out" were the last five words I had anticipated hearing from God one afternoon in October. I had just come from dropping my kids off at their grandparents' house when I made a last-minute decision to hop on the freeway, which was the shortest route to our local Target. Our family had begun homeschooling a month prior, and I was looking forward to a kid-free shopping experience. I had taken this entrance ramp in my car hundreds of times before, so I didn't think twice about flooring the accelerator pedal to get up to highway speed. As I entered the freeway, I surveyed the traffic I was to merge with and saw that I would need to speed up rapidly to get ahead of an approaching semi-truck in the right lane.

To my shock and horror, when I took my foot off the gas pedal, my car kept accelerating! The speed continued climbing up to 80 miles per hour, even with my foot off the accelerator. I laid into my brakes, but there was no drop in speed. That's when I knew I needed to get off the freeway, so I swerved my car to the exit ramp. After trying the emergency brake with the speed only climbing higher, I cried out, "Jesus, help!" When those words rolled off my tongue, I heard a voice behind me say, "Do you trust Me? Janell, you have to jump out."

So, I spun around the corner at the lighted intersection at the end of the exit ramp, and witnesses say I jumped out of the driver's side door onto the pavement. As soon as my body hit the ground, the car accelerated and swerved left, running over my right leg, crossing the median, dashing into oncoming traffic, and hopping the opposite curb, where a large tree stopped it.

Hours later, I found myself in the emergency room. The tiny room where they had put me was empty because of pandemic protocols. Suddenly, my right eye caught sight of someone in the back right corner. And when they started walking toward me, I realized I knew who it was. It was Jesus. My heart knew His presence. He gave me a wink, and then, just as quickly as He had appeared, He vanished.

My injuries were relatively minor, considering what had happened. The nursing staff explained that my nose was broken, and my fingers felt over a dozen metal staples along the ridge of my skull, where dried blood had crusted over my hair in the back of my head. My right leg was in excruciating pain, and my tongue felt parts of my front teeth that were missing, but I was alive! When the hospital discharged me after a few days, they sent me a lengthy list of appointments and a walker.

The first week was probably one of the most challenging weeks of my life. The doctors had explained to me that I had suffered a traumatic brain injury, which left me feeling constantly dizzy, tired, in pain, and unable to handle noise or lights. The second day I was home, I experienced severe whiplash, which was the most excruciating headache I have ever encountered. Then there was my leg that the car had run over; surprisingly, nothing was broken, but there was severe damage to the nerves on my right calf, and the tumble I took jumping out of my car caused a sprain to the ACL under my right knee. It was challenging to get around, and I needed help getting in and out of bed and the chair. I remember laying down, crying, wondering what I had done wrong when immediately the Lord instructed me to grab the blue journal from my nightstand.

When I opened it up to the last entry, my jaw dropped. My hand began to tremble as I read the words my Father had spoken to me the day before my accident. He reminded me there is no shame in suffering—only victory in Jesus. Tears rolled down my cheeks onto the pages as I felt the waterfall of His love pour over my damaged brain and broken body.

A couple of years went by, and everyone witnessed God's healing on the outside of me, but on the inside, memories began to emerge from the depths of my subconscious. I began to struggle with something a therapist later recognized as post-traumatic stress disorder. Whenever I entered a vehicle, blood would start pounding in my ears, my heart would thud in my chest, my hands would shake, my arms would tingle, and my vision would become disfigured, as if I was looking through a fish-eye lens. I felt this urge within me to get out of the car. At the same time, I felt trapped, with no way to escape. It would cause me to clutch the steering wheel, my hands wrapped so tightly around it that my nails would dig into my palms. Breathing would become difficult, which made me cry even harder, and my chest would grow tight as bile rose in my throat.

The worst part is that I would go weeks without a panic attack, only to have it triggered by the memory of jumping out. Shame began to build a fortress in my heart, and there was a part of me that felt utterly abandoned by the Lord. He had healed the rest of my body, but would He recover my memories? Would He take away my fear? Would He calm the raging storm inside of me? It felt like I was in a holding pattern of terror, powerless to land the plane. Then the words of Jesus came into my heart once again: "Janell, who told you that I deserted you? My arms never let you go." With that encounter, everything started to change.

I began to declare God's truth over my life, proclaiming my position as His beloved daughter. The Lord Jesus began to invite me to the secret place, a place where the two of us could come together and meet face-to-face. When I closed my eyes, I began to see Him, just as I had in the ER, and His disposition was always warm toward me. The setting would change frequently. Sometimes, I would sit on a porch swing on a beach with the Father, listening to the waves and letting the tide go over our feet. I would lay my head on His chest, moving in rhythm with the sound of the seashore, and listen to the sound of His heart beating.

There were other times when Jesus would meet me near a river with a tent nearby, His hand beckoning me to go to the water's edge and to go fishing. There were also moments when I would encounter Jesus in a cabin in the woods that overlooked the mountains, each of us holding a warm cup of coffee and breathing in the cool mountain air. With each encounter, layers of intense emotional pain, a sense of abandonment, and fear lifted off, and the enemy stepped back, just as the Lord had promised.

My journey with Jesus didn't stop there. In one particular encounter, He was in the middle of the river, with the water up to His chest, and He was beckoning me to follow Him to the other side. As I put one foot on the water's edge, something remarkable happened. The river suddenly stopped flowing, as if it was held back by an invisible barrier. When the water receded, I saw an iridescent net held by heavenly beings. The path in front of me was bone-dry, and the riverbed to my right looked like it had been dried up for years.

As I got closer to Jesus, I saw Him beckon me with His eyes to look behind, and when I did, I saw thousands of people pursuing the same path I was on. After meeting with the Lord, He commissioned me to write a devotional that would draw suffering saints whom He loves to the place of encounter, where they can follow Jesus and cross the river to take back the ground the enemy had stolen.

My prayer for each of you reading this is that you would feel the Father's love flood your innermost being, disarming the enemy of all his weapons formed against your connection to God. I pray that you develop your secret place with Jesus, where you can experience His pleasure and goodwill toward you. I hope you also develop spiritual ears to discern the sound of the Holy Spirit, who sings songs of deliverance over your life, always guiding you toward Jesus.

Indeed, we can all find a place of safety and security, even in pain and devastating loss, because God told us we can. Psalm 91 describes this place of great intimacy, given to us as our eternal inheritance. There is no fear, no sickness, and no enemy. God's voice brings ceaseless instruction, healing, placement, encouragement, alignment, empowerment, and prosperity to the innermost parts of your being when you meet with Him in this private meeting place. Even if there are days when you come to Him, and you can't *feel* Him or *hear* His voice the way you have in the past, come anyway. Come with thanksgiving, and approach Him with praise. It's time to trust He's there because He said He would be.

BUILDING A DEVOTIONAL TIME WITH THE LORD

This devotional will draw you into having weekly encounters with the Father, Son, and Holy Spirit. I will be sharing the very words that He spoke to me in the middle of my heartache and pain. These prophetic words were given to me with the purpose of sharing them with you, for He is saying the same things over you and your circumstances. Each week has a specific theme and will contain a short letter from the Father, Son, or the Holy Spirit to your fragile heart. Please be free to take this devotional at your own pace. We are not in any rush in this journey, and the Lord is inviting you to come as you are, ready to engage with His presence and His love. If you are going at a daily pace, you will complete this devotional in forty-two days, or six weeks.

TAKING A DEEPER LOOK THROUGH THE BOOK OF JOB

Suffering causes us to question the goodness of God and our place in our relationship with Him. In this place of pain, we have two choices: we can either move slowly *away* from God or draw *closer* to Him. This devotional is for those pursuing the latter choice. As you walk through pain with God, this devotional will release encouragement to protect your connection, challenge you to a place of total surrender, reveal your identity, affirm the terms of your covenant with God, restore your expectation of supernatural support, and prepare your heart for daily encounters with His glorious presence.

The story of Job gives us hope for our restoration, which was paid for with the pain and suffering of Jesus on that old, rugged cross. Jesus died to provide us with an intimate connection to the Father, and He came to restore all the damage that sin's separation has caused. Our surrendered lives are the reward of Christ's sufferings. You are the one Jesus fixed His eyes upon when His back was scourged and His hands were pierced. So, no matter the situation that you are facing, God is drawing you in closer, ready to overwhelm you with His magnificent love. He has the strength you need to keep moving forward as you wait to see the fulfillment of His precious promises.

If you would like to go deeper, at any time during this devotional, you can read the book of Job. You could read the chapter corresponding to each devotional day—forty-two chapters for forty-two days. Reading the book of Job is not a requirement, but it is a helpful companion on the journey through pain with the Lord. Below is the list of chapters in correlation to the devotional weeks and their themes.

Week 1: Days 1–7
Theme: Connection
Bible Reading: Job 1–7

Week 2: Days 8–14
Theme: Surrender
Bible Reading: Job 8–14

Week 3: Days 15–21
Theme: Identity
Bible Reading: Job 15–21

Week 4: Days 22–28
Theme: Covenant
Bible Reading: Job 22–28

Week 5: Days 29–35
Theme: Support
Bible Reading: Job 29–35

Week 6: Days 36–42
Theme: Encounter
Bible Reading: Job 36–42

I don't know what stage you are at in your journey with the Lord—whether in the beginning, middle, or end of a season of suffering. But as Jesus repeatedly proves, *He is our place of safety*. When we go through trials and tribulations in this life, we have a secure promise of Christ, leading us from pain into His redemption. The Lord's kindness will see you through it all, and I am praying that as you read this devotional, you will encounter His presence and power. May your expectation of His light shining through the darkest valley and driest wilderness increase a hundredfold, and may His love bring lifelong transformation to your heart. After reading this devotional, I pray that, like Job, you will stand and say to the Lord, *"Now my eyes see You!"* (Job 42:5).

WEEK 1: CONNECTION

Can anything ever separate us from Christ's love?
Does it mean he no longer loves us if we have trouble or calamity,
or are persecuted, or hungry, or destitute, or in danger, or threatened
with death? ... No, despite all these things, overwhelming
victory is ours through Christ, who loved us.
—Romans 8:35, 37, NLT—

INVITATION: ESTABLISH A CONNECTION TO THE FATHER ON YOUR JOURNEY THROUGH PAIN

On my journey through the wilderness, one of the most brutal battles I had to fight was keeping and building my connection to the *Father.* We all have a supernatural enemy who is after our connection, whispering lies to our minds about God's love for us. Satan sows seeds of suspicion, which can cause us to ponder the following questions:

- Why is this happening?
- Who is to blame?
- Is God withholding something from me?

These questions lead you away from the Lord by slowly stripping away your trust in Him. There is no scarcity in God's love for us, so trusting that promise will be the foundation for our connection with Him.

How we connect with God on an individual level depends on the relationship and the season of life that we are in. You can join Him by enjoying nature and admiring the work of His hands, or you can connect through a workout program at your local fitness center. You can connect with Him while doing dishes, folding laundry, or tidying up the house. You can join the Lord by helping others at your job or while checking out at the grocery store. You can meet with Him by reading His Word and dancing around the kitchen with the worship music playing in the background. Our connection with God should be ongoing because Jesus died to bring us into right relationship with the Father. He built a bridge across the chasm of separation with His blood. May we never forget what it cost Him. The offering of His life grants us the favor of a relationship with the King of the Universe. As His redeemed sons and daughters, let's keep looking for opportunities to grow in our connection with Him.

The following is the Father's love letter to you, His beloved child. As you read it, take His words to heart and receive His strength to keep standing in faith. He invites you to a deeper connection, and He longs for you to come closer to Him.

Beloved,

Your suffering has put My love for you to the ultimate test. I know there has been a growing suspicion of My faithfulness. You have felt abandoned by Me. Beloved, I have watched you. I have cried and yearned desperately for you, knowing you would return to Me someday. In your most intense pain, although you were unaware, I never left your side. Remember, you are a part of Me. How could I ever forget you, beloved? Your name is always on My heart. Every wound of yours became My wound. When you hurt, I hurt also.

The enemy's goal during this season has been to dislodge your trust in Me. He wants to sever our connection; he longs to break us apart. I know there is a part of you that wants resolution. Other pieces of you are still unsure if I am reliable. That is an expected part of our journey together. This place of intimacy that I'm bringing you into requires transparency. I am opening Myself up to you. And you are on your way to discovering My nature and My ways. Beloved, deep parts of your soul long to be revealed, and my Son, Jesus, yearns for you to bring each of those parts to Him. No matter how messy it gets, know that I love all of it. I love even what you call a mess. I am not ashamed of who you are now because I know who I am making you into. Over the next seven days, we are going to connect. I will be there, and you can decide how close you want to come to Me each day. I understand if you wish to keep Me at a distance. But I want you to know that both of My arms are ready to embrace you.

Behold, beloved, I am giving you a seed of faith today. And this seed will cause you to see the truth when you cannot sense it, for it is a supernatural seed. And My faith is given to you to grow into this sweet, aromatic fruit of My Spirit, attracting others to My Son, Jesus. You will not need a lot of faith to remove obstacles; you only need a mustard seed size. You can rely on that. I will be faithful and true because that is who I am for you. On our journey together, you will discover My love and long-suffering faithfulness.

So, beloved, will you let Me grow you up in Christ when you suffer? I have a purpose for it. There is no shame in suffering; instead, there is only victory in Jesus. Watch Me set things right, set all things in order. Every place you will step with Me, we are taking ground, and the enemy is moving back.

Love,
Your Abba Father

Additional Reading Option: Job Chapters 1–7

DAY 1: READY TO RESCUE YOU

Is anyone crying for help? God is listening, ready to rescue you.
If your heart is broken, you'll find God right there;
if you're kicked in the gut, he'll help you catch your
breath. Disciples so often get into trouble;
still, God is there every time.
—Psalm 34:17–19, MSG—

INVITATION: REMEMBER YOUR HISTORY WITH GOD AS YOUR RESCUER

Certain situations leave us feeling metaphorically kicked in the gut. Even as a believer, it can be challenging, in those moments, to recognize God's presence and His compassion toward us. It becomes increasingly difficult when a problem is ongoing, and our prayers seem to be hitting some ceiling. Like in the story of Job, our physical eyes cannot see what is occurring in the supernatural realm. In those moments of impaired vision, we must put our trust in God's promises—despite our emotions and in the middle of harsh circumstances.

One of these promises to grab onto tightly during turbulent circumstances and desperation is the promise that *God will never abandon you.* Would a good father ever reject his children when they come to him with a need? Of course not! God is a good Father, and knowing that aspect of His nature is profoundly significant because it affects our relationship with Him. Jesus was the very first person to reveal God as a Father. His assignment was to unveil the rescuing nature of God, who had existed since before time began.

As a Father, God is here to rescue us from our troubles. The rescue, however, does not always involve God pulling us out of situations. Instead, He often walks with us through the fires and floods of our lives. And in those seasons of anguish, it is foundational for us to grasp the nature of God as our *Abba Father.*

You may have heard God mentioned as *Abba Father* throughout your life—in prayers, at church, in worship songs, or while reading the Bible. However, this title of *Abba Father* is found in Scripture a total of three times (Mark 14:36, Romans 8:15, and Galatians 4:6). Some would argue that Abba is the same word as Father, but if that were true, what would be the rationale for Jesus and Paul's redundancy? Is it possible that the word *Abba* has a different meaning than *Father?*

The New Testament was written in Greek, but Abba is not a Greek word; instead, it is an Aramaic word transliterated into Greek letters. *Abba* is the Aramaic word for "father." *Abba* is also a word used for devotion, a term of endearment. Therefore, some have concluded that *Abba*'s new translation could be "Daddy" or "Papa." The Lord calls us into divine intimacy, calling Him "Abba, our beloved Father."

There are two traits of God's role as a father. *Abba* is the loving, endearing, accepting, and healing trait of God. The *Father* is the authoritative trait of God, one who draws boundaries and provides guidance and discipline. Only knowing God as Abba can lead us into lawlessness because we can only see God as accepting; at the same time, only knowing Him as Father can lead us into legalism.[1]

When believers only know God as the Father who creates boundaries, their relationship with Him will reflect that of being a rule follower, which becomes transactional instead of relational. How we know God does not change Him, but it changes us. How we see God affects everything we do, and we need both eyes functioning together to view our Abba Father properly. He is always eager and willing to respond to our cries, even before we utter words. The psalm above illustrates how deeply involved our Abba Father desires to be with us in the pain we go through. Jesus cried out to God as Abba Father when He was at His weakest moment in the Garden of Gethsemane. God answered His cry by sending angels to strengthen Him so that He could endure the suffering of the cross. When Job cried out for a redeemer, the Father responded with abundant love and redemption. In the presence of our pain, our hearts require the same assurance that God is our rescuer.

Another foundational truth that shapes our view of God, who will always rescue us, is that God does not play favorites. Peter concluded this in his journey: *"I now realize how true it is that God does not show favoritism"* (Acts 10:33–35, NIV). God cares profoundly about the small and the big things in our lives because He loves us. Just as an earthly dad would be proud enough to hang his young son's painting of smudges and scratches on the fridge, God is deeply involved in the things that matter most to you.

There is good news today for you in the midst of pain. God is ready to respond to your cries before you utter a word. Look at Psalm 34:17–19 again to grasp how deeply involved the Lord desires to be in your life.

REFLECTION

To what degree does my heart see God as my rescuer?

PRAYER

Father, today, I desire to see You as my rescuer. Please show me situations in my past where You have rescued me, helping me get through some hard things. Help me to remember our history together. You have always been there, and Your Word says You will never leave me. Help me to trust You as a rescuer while I walk through this season of pain.

ACTIVATION

Think of one time God rescued you. Thank Him and praise Him that He will always come through for you!

DAY 2: THE MIND OF CHRIST

WE POSSESS CHRIST'S PERCEPTIONS.

We possess Christ's perceptions.
—1 Corinthians 2:16, TPT—

INVITATION: THINK LIKE CHRIST

We possess something Job never had: a new and better covenant. Jesus replaced the old one with one that is established on better promises. It is a beautiful pledge full of innumerable benefits and blessings, and yet so many have entered this covenant unaware of what those promises are. As you progress in your relationship with God, you will discover His promises are the language of love between you and Him. And this discovery is designed to teach you His superior thoughts and miraculous ways.

On this journey of discovery and training, we need a revelation of what belongs to each of us through the new blood covenant. One of those benefits received from the moment of our salvation is the mind of Christ. When we said yes to Jesus, we received a *"helmet of salvation"* (Ephesians 6:17). This helmet serves many profound purposes, including its protection from the lies of the enemy by intercepting fear in our thoughts.

Paul demonstrated how this supernatural helmet operates in his letter to the church in Corinth. He stated, *"Someone living on an entirely human level rejects the revelations of God's Spirit, for they make no sense to him. He can't understand the revelations of the Spirit because they are only discovered by the illumination of the Spirit. Those who live in the Spirit are able to carefully evaluate all things, and they are subject to the scrutiny of no one but God"* (1 Corinthians 2:14–15, TPT). The passage above means that part of our salvation involves transforming thinking habits to match God's narrative over our lives. This transformation is not intellectually or logically obtained because God is not speaking to our heads. The Spirit of God would never speak to the most resistant part of us; instead, He first speaks to our hearts. And from the heart flows the wellspring of His life in us. His Word impressed upon our hearts becomes the new vocabulary in our minds. God has given us His helmet to protect us from inferior thoughts, and we have also been given an overcoming Spirit that intercepts fear, casting it to the feet of Jesus.

Although fear remains on this side of Heaven, we have the responsibility to stop that anxiety from turning into a lifestyle. While many deny the reality of warfare, we know this is not the truth. Why would Paul instruct us to put on the armor of God if there was no longer any threat? Christ has given us victory, but we must *enforce* His victory on an already defeated enemy. We must never assume that we receive immunity from the works of Satan after accepting Christ. We are not immune to temptations, trials, and tribulations, and until we are glorified with Christ, we will encounter resistance.

This demonic resistance we face can show up in our thought lives. The devil is persistent in his quest to steal, kill, and destroy the calling and purpose of every believer. The more you obey and serve Christ, the more intense the warfare will get over your mind until you overcome inferior thoughts with Christ, pulling down strongholds of the mind. However, when reacting to an error in our thinking, we can unknowingly make another by focusing on our opponent. Instead, we must focus on the terms of our covenant with God through Jesus Christ. Paul instructed us to put on the helmet of salvation, but what does it look like to heed Paul's directive in our lives?

Steps to Putting on Your Helmet:

1. Remember your salvation – We find protection from lies by remembering what we are saved or rescued from. Jesus has delivered us from the power of sin, shame, the devil, and every curse. When we practice remembering how Christ has saved us, it releases supernatural power for Him to rescue us again.
2. Filter your thoughts – We can ask God to reveal lies we have believed, since many lies are hidden. When God reveals a lie, we can demolish it by breaking our agreement and replacing it with God's words.
3. Proclaim the words of Jesus – The apostle Paul wrote, *"Faith comes from hearing, and hearing through the word of Christ"* (Romans 10:17, ESV). When we speak what Christ said out loud, we hear, and it builds our faith.

We live an abundant life when we protect our minds, accepting all the benefits of the gospel of Jesus. If Jesus came to offer us an abundant life, why would we choose to live on less than good enough? The price that Jesus paid was enough for us to live in abundance. He died to save our souls from sin, our minds from fear, and our bodies from infirmity. Jesus's suffering provided a piece of God's armor that is essential in our daily walk with Him; however, it does us no good unless we put it on daily.

In addition to reflecting and decreeing our salvation, we have another advantage: we can know what Jesus knew on earth. There were three specific things that Jesus knew, and they were the will of His Father, how to partner with the Kingdom realm, and how to defeat the works of the devil. We possess the ability to think like that. The Lord designed us to know the will of our heavenly Father. God also placed within us the capability to initiate Kingdom culture on earth, and He most certainly calls His people to carry on what Jesus did by defeating the works of the devil.

REFLECTION

Review the "Steps to Putting on Your Helmet" again. Which one of those steps needs my focus?

PRAYER

Jesus, what lies have I believed about having a mind of Christ?

[Wait for the Lord to reveal the lie.]

Jesus, thank You for exposing that lie. I break the agreement with that lie and ask for Your forgiveness. Now, what truth do You want me to believe?

[Wait for the Lord to reveal the truth.]

Thank You, Jesus, for giving me a revelation of truth. I receive that truth by faith.

ACTIVATION

Close your eyes and picture a helmet on your head, one strong enough to protect you against fiery darts. Then say out loud, "I have the mind of Christ!" Do this daily to remind yourself of the benefit of belonging to Jesus and possessing His thoughts!

DAY 3: UNLIMITED ABUNDANCE

The thief comes only in order to steal and kill and destroy. I came that they may have and enjoy life, and have it in abundance [to the full, till it overflows].
—John 10:10, AMP—

INVITATION: EXCHANGE A POVERTY MINDSET FOR AN ABUNDANCE MINDSET

Have you ever been afraid of running out of something? Many of us subconsciously operate under the assumption of scarcity. This fear of not having enough goes past tangible items like food or money. We can also cultivate the fear of running short of grace, using all of God's love and affection as if we could exhaust His resources. Or we can operate with the perspective that God is only willing to heal us a few times, so we stop running to Him for healing and accept our infirmities as His will. Many of us have built these subconscious mental museums devoted to scarcity when we did not have all that we expected in front of our physical eyes.

Doing so, we can consequently restrict what God can do in assumed shortage because of our thought life.

Do you remember when Jesus showed up in a time of shortage in the Bible? The disciples held on to what they could see with their physical eyes and reported, *"All we have are five loaves of bread and two fish"* (Matthew 14:17, MSG). The resources they had did not match up with the need, right? However, Jesus exposed them to a new perspective. He showed them how to look at this scarcity through the eyes of God, and they became witnesses to the overflow of the Father. Jesus, the perfect expression of the Father, never did anything outside of God's will. From that understanding of His identity, we can conclude that God wants us to become His stewards of overflow.

Looking through the lens of *scarcity* attracts fear and anxiety. An attitude of lack is not for a disciple of Jesus. So, how do we move out of this mindset? The first thing we must do is recognize the position we are taking in prayer. Jesus commissioned us to pray in His authority. He demonstrated how to recognize a need as an opportunity to bring God's redemptive plan. He knew that in prayer, all things are possible. Prayer gives us access to a God who is above it all. Therefore, the position we take in prayer makes a difference. We are not powerless, for Heaven has all the resources we need for each problem we encounter. When we pray from this posture, fear is no longer part of the equation. This abundance mindset of overflow is our responsibility to steward, knowing the will of God for our lives. We must agree to become a people who co-labor with Heaven to bring God's Kingdom to earth.

The second step to moving out of a mindset of lack is exchanging a *scarcity* approach for a *stewardship* approach. We are all given resources with the expectation from the Lord that we will steward all that the Father has generously put into our hands. In the story of the talents, Jesus revealed that God gives resources to people with an expectation of multiplication. God asks, "What do you have?" because He wants to perform miracles of overflow in our lives. On our own, it will never add up, but when we partner with God, we will have enough left to share with others. Overflow is for His glory.

We serve a God with no limits! If God asks you to do something, and you observe the little you *see*, remind yourself of the loaves and fish miracle. We serve a God who pours out more than we can contain in our earthly vessels. As He pours into us, we overflow and pour into others. The story of Job is an example of this unlimited abundance, and it reveals that if we lose everything, God can redeem every wound, trauma, and injury. In the end, Job said, *"I know that my redeemer lives, and that in the end he will stand on the earth. And after my skin has been destroyed, yet in my flesh I will see God; I myself will see him with my own eyes—I, and not another"* (Job 19:25–27, NIV). This beautiful truth of the gospel is one that many miss, but not you. You are discovering through the Spirit of God that He is not tightfisted. You can never exhaust God's resources. He is looking for you to become a willing vessel, always asking for more of Him!

REFLECTION

Do I sense God inviting me to accept this limitless abundance?

Is there anything that is hindering me from putting on this new lens?

What does God want to multiply in my life (God's love, favor, grace, wisdom)?

PRAYER

Father, thank You for giving me all I need to overflow. Open my eyes so I can see what is in my heavenly account. Help me to become a better steward of Your resources.

ACTIVATION

Picture yourself holding a pair of glasses with an outdated prescription. These glasses represent your old scarcity mindset. Ask Jesus to come and take this lens of lack from you. After releasing it to Him, ask Jesus to give you a lens of abundance and overflow. Let Him reveal what this new lens looks like. Whatever He shows you, write it down in a journal. Recording what you experienced will help reinforce this supernatural exchange.

DAY 4: WORD OF TRUTH

Always be eager to present yourself before God as a perfect and mature minister, without shame, as one who correctly explains the Word of Truth.
—2 Timothy 2:15, TPT—

INVITATION: ALLOW GOD'S WRITTEN AND SPOKEN WORD OF TRUTH TO BE PLANTED IN YOUR HEART THROUGH EACH TRIAL

As a follower of Jesus, we are called to a higher level of excellence, boldly proclaiming the *Word of Truth*. You may be wondering at this point if God is holding us to the same standards as Paul had for Timothy. While there is a higher standard for those in a leadership role in the church, Jesus has commanded all His followers to spread the good news of the gospel, His truth. The problem is the enemy has deceived many into believing that only certain people are called into ministry. If we believe that lie, it will pollute what the *Word of Truth* says about our role as gospel ministers. So, what does God say about our ministry?

> *But you are God's chosen treasure—priests who are kings, a spiritual "nation" set apart as God's devoted ones. He called you out of darkness to experience his marvelous light, and now he claims you as his very own. He did this so that you would broadcast his glorious wonders throughout the world.*
>
> —1 PETER 2:9, TPT

According to the *Word of Truth*, each child of God is a priest and king, God's unique and special treasure of great importance. Therefore, you are His priest and, as such, are called to know the *Word of Truth* enough to be able to explain it to unbelievers. But before the intimidation seeps in, remember that whenever God asks something of us, He provides the necessary tools for us to accomplish it. Moses was a prime example of someone initially intimidated by the mission God called him to. He felt unequipped to lead the Israelites out of slavery, but God tenderly assured Moses that he had everything needed to complete the task.

Another example is the prophet Jeremiah. He told God that he did not have what it took to be a prophet because of his age, but God revealed to Jeremiah that his age would not prevent him from carrying God's *Word of Truth* to the nation of Israel. Like Moses and Jeremiah, God desires for all of His children to accept what He has given to us despite any of our fleshly insufficiencies. We can trust that God equips the called.

We are called to share the message of God's *Word of Truth*, and we can trust that He will equip us with the necessary tools and resources to fulfill that calling, including His grace and guidance. It is through His divine power and wisdom that we can spread His message with clarity, conviction, and compassion, touching the hearts and minds of those who hear it. Scripture says, *"God is able to make all grace abound to you, so that having all sufficiency in all things at all times, you may abound in every good work"* (2 Corinthians 9:8, ESV). Because we are called and equipped, we can become partners with God to accomplish our purpose of carrying His Word of Truth in our hearts. In the story of

Job, he was searching for the truth, but all he found were untrue accusations from his close friends until the Lord showed up. We can avoid becoming like Job's friends, whom he ended up referring to as *worthless physicians,* when we partner with God's truth. Our partnership begins with immersing ourselves in the Bible and allowing the Holy Spirit to penetrate the truth of God's Word into our hearts.

REFLECTION

What *Word of Truth* does the Lord want to grow inside of my heart? It could be a single word, phrase, or Scripture to meditate on.

Examples:

1. *"You, O Lord, are a shield about me, my glory, and the lifter of my head"* (Psalm 3:3).
2. "Liberty."[1]
3. "When I stand in Your love, *all* fear has to go!"[2]

PRAYER

Father, I love Your Word of Truth. *Thank You for equipping me with what I need to be a minister of Your truth. Please enlarge my heart today so I can receive the revelation of Your* Word of Truth *that You have already deposited into me as a seed. Show me how to hide Your Word in my heart so that it develops strong roots, and teach me how to speak the truth to myself and others who need encouragement.*

ACTIVATION

Ask the Lord what part of His *Word of Truth* He wants to plant in you. Is there a Scripture or a promise that He wants you to meditate on during this season? Whatever He gives you, write it down and come back to it often.

DAY 5: YOUR REWARDER

And it is impossible to please God without faith.
Anyone who wants to come to him must believe that
God exists and that he rewards those who sincerely seek him.
—Hebrews 11:6, NLT—

INVITATION: BEGIN SEEKING GOD, TRUSTING THAT HE WILL REWARD YOUR PURSUIT OF HIM

God's praise of Job's integrity provoked an attack against *God's integrity*. God was speaking as a proud papa would brag about his son's performance on the baseball field. This conversation reveals God's ultimate desire to connect with us. However, Satan disagreed and began to challenge God's ways. He told God that Job's integrity was *bought* by all the blessings God had given him. In other words, the enemy accused God of buying His friends. If that were true, our relationship with God would be superficial.

If we only served God to get things from Him, there could never be true intimacy. Having a relationship with God is what sets Christianity apart from all religions. The Lord doesn't love us for what we can give Him. He didn't love Job because He was a righteous and upright man. God loved Job simply because Job was *a son*. When the enemy comes to us with an accusation against God, it is usually related to His fatherhood. We must believe the revealed truth of God's character with an expectation that He will reveal more of Himself to us, because God is a rewarder of those who seek Him.

The closer our intimacy is with the Lord, the more evident this characteristic of Him will be for us. God created us to experience constant connection with Him, provided for us by the generosity of His grace. Jesus repaired what sin had broken and what good works could never attain. And God rewarded Jesus for His sufferings on the cross by adopting us into His family.

The Lord rewards us for responding to the promptings of His Spirit, drawing us closer to Jesus Christ. It is important to note that the rewards spoken of in this passage of Scripture are for those who *"diligently seek Him."* The words diligently and seek come from the Greek word *ekzeteo,* which means to investigate or crave.[1] So, to seek diligently after God means that we sincerely crave a connection with Him, for all relationships are built on that bond, where both parties are wanting to connect.

God created a desire in you to *find Him,* and He looks forward to your discovery of who He is. Just like a father finds joy in his child finding all the Easter eggs they had carefully hidden around the yard, your Father delights in you finding revelations of His nature and goodness. You glorify God by diligently seeking Him throughout your day, inviting Him to be a part of your everyday life, even in the most mundane situations.

Jesus also shows us the reward of seeking the Lord in the book of Matthew: *"Ask and it will be given to you; seek and you will find; knock and the door will be opened to you. For everyone who asks receives; the one who seeks finds; and to the one who knocks, the door will be opened"* (Matthew 7:7–8, NIV). Our reward becomes part of His reward, which brings

Him great joy. However, there are times in life when God will remove things, or strip away relationships, roles, positions, and things you may be relying on, so that there are no distractions from Him. He will hide you so you can discover more of Him. If that's where you are right now, take heart! God is providing a place of discovery for you, full of His goodness. This season of discovery plays a unique role in your development. It comes when God wants to *build something new* in your heart. Remember, He's only hiding for you to discover! He is building history with you. Proverbs 25:2 says, *"It is the glory of God to conceal things, but the glory of kings is to search things out"* (ESV). God's glory is in the *concealing*, and our glory is in the *searching*, so let's seek to know more about our glorious Rewarder.

REFLECTION

What part of God's character does He want me to discover in this season? (Some examples of attributes are His generosity, patience, comfort, gentleness, holiness, wisdom, goodness, power, grace, glory, justice, and many more.)

PRAYER

Father God, thank You for offering me a love that wants connection. I desire to know You as a rewarder, and I'm willing to lay aside other things in my life to seek You diligently. Please show me what to lay down in this season of discovery. Thank You for guiding me on this quest to discover more of You.

ACTIVATION

Whatever He shows you in prayer, seek to know that part of Him by looking for those attributes in His Word and asking Him questions along the way. You are on your way to discovering a new piece of God's nature! Hallelujah!

DAY 6: ENTWINING YOUR HEART

Don't give up; don't be impatient; be entwined as one with the Lord. Be brave and courageous, and never lose hope. Yes, keep on waiting—for he will never disappoint you!"
—Psalm 27:14, TPT—

INVITATION: PURSUE GOD'S HEART BY WAITING IN HIS PRESENCE

Throughout the book of Job, his friends took turns hurling accusations against him. It becomes obvious that Job was struggling as the time progressed. It is difficult to remain steadfast during unfair allegations. Hopefully, you have never received the same kind of accusations as Job, but no doubt we have all experienced an *accuser of the brethren* in this area.[1] The enemy loves to bring up our past, especially the sins that God has already forgiven, which died with Jesus on the cross at Calvary. How can we remain steadfast and focused on Jesus and our purpose when accusations are hurled in our faces day and night?

Regarding any false accusations, our responsibility is not to defend ourselves but to run to God, letting Jesus rise as our defense attorney. It is not our good works that will save our spiritual reputation; instead, it is the righteousness of Jesus Christ that testifies our innocence. Satan is banking on us not understanding our position as sons and daughters of God who have been made clean by the blood of Jesus. Our enemy is hoping that we will surrender our minds and our imaginations to *him* by failing to guard the gates of our hearts and minds.

Our accuser is also stealthy, playing the game carefully so that his presence in our minds goes unnoticed. If a thought is obviously from him, we won't receive it, so he must pervert and corrupt what God says to draw us away from the Lord. How do we shut off this noise of our accuser? How do we protect ourselves from being overcome by his or others' accusations? How does a person keep *peace* in the middle of *chaos*?

The book of Isaiah tells us that peace is a result of keeping our focus fixed on God: *"You keep him in perfect peace whose mind is stayed on you, because he trusts in you"* (Isaiah 26:3, ESV). The Passion Translation says it a little differently: *"Perfect, absolute peace surrounds those whose imaginations are consumed with you; they confidently trust in you."* In studying the human mind, we know that imagination is the framework for our perceived realities. We must fully surrender our imaginations to the Lord. Our submission to allow that inward transformation by the Holy Spirit can reform how we think, making our imaginations holy.

Let's pause for a moment and reflect on the power that our imaginations have over our lives. Imaginations originate in our souls, influenced by whatever we feed it with. If we feed our flesh, our souls will follow suit. Feeding our flesh looks like concentrating all of our attention on fear and managing our imaginations in a way that keeps us safe from transformation. However, if we feed our spirits, our souls will follow, thus maturing our faith.

God has given us His Spirit to lead our thoughts so that we can grow and mature in Christ. He knows that our actions are affected by our imaginations, so we must learn to bring our feelings before His throne of grace, allowing Him to take the lead. Our imaginations will eventually affect the soil of our hearts, which is where the life of Christ flows from. So, we need to keep our imaginations focused on God, and when we do, it will become easier for us to follow the ways of God's heart.

The word entwine appears later in the book of Isaiah: "*Yes, we will follow your ways, Lord Yahweh, and entwine our hearts with yours*" (Isaiah 26:8, TPT). When thinking of the word entwine, we can picture a rope. The Hebrew word *quavah* (the root word for "rope") means "to wait, to entwine."[2] Waiting on God, or entwining our hearts to His, suggests that we are interlocking our hearts to God's character and the promises He has made. The interlocking of our hearts is the yoke Jesus talked about in Matthew 11. His yoke is *easy*. Taking on Jesus's yoke, or following what He says, is the same as entwining our hearts to God.

Waiting on the Lord is never a passive thing! Instead, it is an active pursuit, full of hope with an expectation of connection. We can tune out the accuser's voice by keeping our eyes fixed on who God is for us and all He has promised us through Christ Jesus, our Lord. When Jesus becomes our focus, peace is automatic. God's peace results from an imagination fully surrendered to Him and a heart braided with His heart during the chaos and impossible-seeming situations.

REFLECTION

How does God want me to pursue His heart today? (Through soaking in His presence? Meditating on a specific psalm? Entering into a time of worship or focusing on a particular aspect of God's heart?) Ask Him to show you how He wants to be pursued today.

PRAYER

Lord, thank You for always showing me kindness. Today, I want to follow Your heart. Show me the way so I can remain close to You in this season of waiting. Strengthen me by Your precious Spirit.

ACTIVATION

Place both of your hands on your heart and make this declaration: "My heart is pursuing the heart of Yahweh!"

DAY 7: BE ALERT

Be sober-minded; be watchful.
Your adversary the devil prowls around like
a roaring lion, seeking someone to devour.
—1 Peter 5:8, ESV—

INVITATION: BECOME ALERT TO WHAT IS INFLUENCING YOUR HEART

God designed us to look like Him, and our calling in this life is to represent Him. In the story of Job, we see a man *reflecting* God's character. Job chose to set himself apart and live the way that God wanted him to live. It was that reflection of God that had brought about a lawsuit in Heaven. Satan is mentioned in the New Testament with the word *antidikos,* which is a legal term for "one who brings a lawsuit."[1] Satan was making accusations against *the way God chose to run the universe,* but he was also making accusations against Job's *motives*. He claimed that Job only followed God's ways because there was a hedge of protection around him. He wanted to prove to God that Job did not love Him for who He was but for the blessings and the favor God had brought into Job's life.

In the Scripture above the passage, Peter suggested that Satan is still roaming to and fro across the earth, seeking to steal, kill, and destroy. Peter knew this from personal experience, for Jesus had shared how Satan asked to sift him like wheat.[2] In Peter's failures, Jesus brought *redemption* and *renewal*, restoring him to the right relationship with God. This testimony of mercy and grace runs parallel to the story of Job, and it reminds us that God has a redemptive plan amid any attack in our lives.

Even though Satan is defeated, we must *stand against him*. We have already chosen to be on God's side in a supernatural war, and Jesus has called us to take ground for the Kingdom of Heaven. We cannot take ground without authority, and the cross provides that authority. As sons and daughters of God, we must learn how to *fight* the roaring lion. How do we do this? The first battle we fight is *inward* (in our hearts and minds), and we must enforce Christ's victory there before engaging in any *outward* battle. We need to know how to fight from a position of victory.

The Scripture above also tells us to be watchful or sober-minded. That means that we have a responsibility to watch over who or what *influences* our lives. We must watch over the influences of our hearts, bringing all of our cares and worries to the Lord. Peter knew that Satan was out to corrupt the hearts of men and women and that he could only do that through influencing them in subtle ways.

Our souls require Christ's redemption, and Jesus is restoring the deepest parts of us so we can be free of sin's corruption. The inward battle we must face includes giving the Spirit of God the right to lead our emotions, thoughts, imaginations, motives, dreams, and desires. Our defensive strategy against the enemy is to *reject rebellion* by *submitting* ourselves to the Lord.

Before Peter compared the enemy to a roaring lion, he challenged us to do two things: we must *humble* ourselves before the Lord, and we must cast our anxieties onto Jesus. Humility protects us from the emotions of pride and fear. When they are left to roam free, it will corrupt our hearts and lead us away from God. A relationship with God is crucial because His Spirit can see the things hidden from our sight. With Jesus, we are discovering how to live *Spirit-led* instead of *soul-driven,* where all of our emotions are learning to submit to His Lordship.

Not only do we reject rebellion by surrendering to God, but we also must take an *offensive* stance by enforcing what Jesus did for us on the cross. Paul encouraged us to embrace our liberty in Christ from Satan's schemes as a lifestyle of freedom. He urged us to stand firm, not allowing ourselves to be burdened again by the yoke of slavery.[3] Jesus is calling you to take a strong defensive position and to be alert to His Spirit, which will warn you of any influence outside His Lordship. He is training you to automatically reject what does not come from Him, all so that you can move upon His path of grace, taking ground for His Kingdom.

REFLECTION

What is dominating my thought life (fear, anger, self-pity, a sense of worthlessness, shame)?

Ask Jesus to reveal where He wants to permeate your heart with His influence.

PRAYER

Jesus, I admit that I need Your help today. I am inviting You to show Yourself strong in all of my weak areas. Show me what I need to bring to You today. Remove any secret areas of corruption in my heart. Light up my heart with Your love! Thank You, Jesus, for giving me victory over every scheme of Satan. In You, I will overcome!

ACTIVATION

It is our responsibility to be vigilant and aware of the things that are impacting our hearts and minds. What are some things Satan, the roaring lion, is throwing out to you as bait (pride, shame, anxiety)? Lay whatever it is the Lord reveals to you down at the feet of Jesus, and turn your face toward Him. Give Jesus Lordship over all your emotions, thoughts, imaginations, motives, dreams, and desires. Invite His Spirit's influence over your heart and keep watch.

WEEK 2: SURRENDER

Trust in the L*ORD* *with all your heart, and do not lean on your own understanding. In all your ways, acknowledge him, and he will make straight your paths. Be not wise in your own eyes; fear the* L*ORD*, *and turn away from evil. It will be healing to your flesh and refreshment to your bones."*
—Proverbs 3:5–8, ESV—

INVITATION: LAY MORE OF YOURSELF DOWN AT THE FEET OF JESUS, GIVING HIM PERMISSION TO MOVE THROUGH YOU

What frightens the enemy more than anything is a person who has surrendered every part of their heart to the Lord, because a person who has submitted their ways to God threatens the works of darkness. Complete surrender may be easier said than done, but God makes it possible. The great benefit of surrender is that Jesus will give you more of Himself in return. When we lay down our right to run our lives, we can stay on a straight path, avoiding pitfalls.

This week, we will learn how to come to God with our questions, striving, unbelief, will, perception, feelings, and earthly comfort. That may feel scary to let things go, but the freedom you will receive from it will far outweigh any temporary distress. God wants you to know that He has placed you in the *driver's seat.* He won't grab the wheel from you and take over completely. We were created to work alongside God. He does not require us to work independently of Him, nor has it been about Him doing everything for us. It must be your decision to invite His direction into your journey. You are in good hands when you allow God to lead and guide your life, even when you encounter something new on the road.

The following letter is from the Father. Read it as a beloved child, knowing that His plans for your life are much better than the ones in your head. It is always safe to trust the Lord, even when we are unaware of the path He has us on. God has promised us that our surrender will lead to *healing* and *refreshment.*

Beloved,

The new place that I am leading you to is for your blessing, not your calamity. There are parts of your heart that remain suspicious of My good intentions. Your soul tries to protect you, but it was never meant to be in the lead. If you allow those parts to manage more and more of your inner world, they will slow down and even stop your spiritual development. My child, there is a better way in the Spirit. My Spirit will stay close to you, instructing and guiding you along the way, leading you toward My redemption with My eyes. Will you give Me the right to develop you? My desire is knocking at the door of your heart.

Beloved, do not be governed by past failures or past events. I declare this is a new day for you! It is time for you to increase the speed of your response. Say yes, beloved! Say yes, and come to Me. Don't hang back, for there is no risk to you if you come. There is only risk in the place of speculation. So, don't allow your caution to deny My perfect will.

There is always a better way, My child. Over the next seven days, we will connect, and I will teach you how to lay down everything restraining your development. I want to teach you how to come to Me, for I have built a place of meeting inside you, which is the sanctuary of our connection. Just as I came upon the altar in the Tabernacle, I will come upon the altar of your heart. Anything you let go of, I will take from you. And through Me, you will receive great strength.

So, come to me with thanksgiving and rejoicing because those are how you will both access and appropriate My nature and My desire. Childlike worship is your key to silencing the madness of those who oppose you, for I am building a stronghold with your praises. Precious one, lay your sacrifices of worship on the altar of your heart so that My fire can come upon it.

My Son, Jesus, will be there with you amid the flames. He will help you to walk through the fire of affliction and come out strengthened, full of courage. And I will bless your name, and I will make your name great because of your relationship with My Son. I prophesy over you today that you will be free indeed! I have knitted you together to fit into My perfect plan, to fulfill My designed purpose. And someday, you will stand and say to those around you, "What the enemy meant for evil, God has caused it all to work for good!"

Love,
Your Abba Father

Additional Reading Option: Job Chapters 8–14

DAY 8: STEADFAST

For you know that the testing
of your faith produces steadfastness.
—James 1:4, ESV—

INVITATION: SURRENDER YOUR "WHY" QUESTION TO REMAIN STEADFAST

The testing of our faith has the potential to produce something called steadfastness. In other translations, the words used instead of steadfastness are *patience* (NKJV) and *endurance* (AMP). The Merriam-Webster dictionary defines steadfastness as "firmly fixed in place: immovable."[1] James was not talking about our physical status here but our spiritual one. When the testing of our faith comes, it is essential that we hold our ground and do not shy away from letting God develop us. But what is God developing?

Love is what Jesus planted in you when you received Him at your salvation, and *His love* is what is being developed in you until it reaches its full maturity at His coming. We must remember that we are a product of God's love, made in His likeness, to reveal Him in the earthly realm. What a high calling we have in Christ: to love God, to love others, and to love ourselves! Jesus told us that the world will recognize who we belong to by our love.[2] Therefore, when we go through trials and testing, God's love is ready to transform more of us into Christ.

The love of God is what is really on trial in the case of this story of Job. Satan challenged the way God was running His universe and told God that His image-bearers only reflected Him because He had put up a hedge of protection around them, keeping them from experiencing loss, pain, and disappointment. In the end, we see the Lord restore Job, and that testimony of restoration is the hope that will hold us through all the suffering we encounter as we develop in our maturity as sons and daughters of God. Jesus died to give us a *better* covenant built upon *better* promises, with our hope fixed on total redemption and restoration.

The apostle Paul reassured us, *"We are troubled on every side, yet not distressed; we are perplexed, but not in despair; Persecuted, but not forsaken; cast down, but not destroyed"* (2 Corinthians 4:8–9, KJV). Trouble, perplexion, persecution, and humility are an essential part of our development. When we see those things as opportunities to *embrace* instead of something to run away from, we will see the faithful presence of God and become purified, maturing in His love and developing more of Christ's characteristics. But, because of free will, we have a choice during our development: we can allow the Lord to form us into someone who is steadfast, or we can walk around in the wilderness for forty years, like the Israelites who never reached the promised land.

James called us to allow testing to do its work, which is a challenging task. Reflecting on your trials, have you ever asked God why He allowed them to happen to you? It is easy to get stuck in this desire to know why bad things happen, but Jesus wants to take us out of that roundabout (that leads to nowhere), and He wants to pull us in a new direction. Pain always has a purpose in Christ, and that purpose is taking you from faith to greater faith and from glory to greater glory. If you allow Him to, Jesus can take you, like Joseph, from a pit to a palace!

Asking God *why* is normal, but there is a better question to ask the Lord through our season of suffering. That question is, *what is this for?* This question will change your life and keep you from staying in a pit or the wilderness. We were created for the promised land, but to get there, we must go through a wilderness season. Jesus wants to take us from a place of *coping* to a place of *conquering*! Conquering begins by breaking any lingering trace of a victimhood mentality and claiming our victory through Christ.

Today, God is inviting you to surrender your old life, old ways, and old habits so that He can start developing you into a person who reflects the steadfast love of Christ, immovable in your devotion to Him. Jesus told us that *"every persistent one will get what he asks for"* (Matthew 7:8, TPT). We see the testimony of the following three women's persistence, or steadfastness, in the Gospels: the persistent widow who kept bringing her case before the judge until he gave her justice,[3] the woman with the issue of blood who persistently reached out to her healer,[4] and the mother who contended with Jesus for her son's deliverance.[5] These women had to remain steadfast to keep persisting. Like them, you must decide to keep trusting God and keep standing on His promises throughout the tests that come in your life. Choose this day to surrender your need to know why and trust Him.

REFLECTION

What "why" question can I lay down at the foot of the cross today?

What question does God want me to replace it with?

PRAYER

Lord, I am choosing to trust You. I surrender my "why" question and allow You to develop me today through Your precious Spirit. Help me to remain steadfast and persistent until I reach the end of this season with Your banner of victory!

ACTIVATION

Release this prophetic declaration over yourself today: "I am remaining steadfast in my faith!"

DAY 9: PORTAL TO GOD'S POWER

So I'm not defeated by my weakness, but delighted!
For when I feel my weakness and endure
mistreatment—when I'm surrounded with troubles on
every side and face persecution because of my love for
Christ—I am made yet stronger. For my weakness
becomes a portal to God's power.
—2 Corinthians 12:10, TPT—

INVITATION: SURRENDER STRIVING IN THE FLESH AND BEGIN THE JOURNEY OF RESTING IN THE SPIRIT

Have you ever had a time in your life where you felt like you were holding dozens of breakable plates, knowing that the strength you had to hold them up would eventually crumble and everything would come crashing down? We have all had these breaking points where we drop one plate after the other. There is nothing like losing control while you are losing control! It is like being on a figurative runaway freight train, going so fast that no matter how hard you try to slow down, it seems like there is nothing you can do to stop it.

Those times of weakness are complicated, and most want to retreat somewhere and bandage their battle wounds. In moments where we are trying to maintain control in our flesh, in *our strength,* we need to remember the One who holds us and never lets go. Even when we are falling apart, Jesus is there with His love so that we can encounter a sufficiency of grace that fills our weaknesses with *His strength* and *power.*

It can be easy to lose sight of our place in the Kingdom of Heaven when we don't feel strong or powerful enough in life's circumstances. We need reminders of our placement. God has *seated us with him in the heavenly places in Christ Jesus,*[1] who is *far above principalities and powers of darkness.*[2] In Christ, we are seated in heavenly places with Him, who is above any other authority. Knowing our position in Christ pushes us from feeling helpless and alone to feeling cared for and loved.

There is grace from God for *your* race or the ministry that God has called you to. And ministry—of the purest kind—is not about impressing others with a perfect life, free of mistakes. It is not about keeping up appearances or maintaining a flawless reputation. Ministry is about living unafraid of exposure to our hidden imperfections while permitting others to do the same. We are called to an authentic lifestyle in Christ, not a "performance-based Christianity." We are all fellow strugglers and faith wrestlers who are never exempt from making mistakes in life. In that case, let's keep our arms linked, delivering grace to one another as Christ has poured out His undeserved grace on us. Why? Because we have a God who says we are enough just as we are. Weaknesses and all, we are all portals to God's power.

Because we are designed to have permanent access to God's power and strength, we can be *delighted* in our weaknesses and see them as *opportunities* to watch God become strong in our lives. It is all about having the proper perspective. Weakness does not tarnish or diminish our value because our worth is not in *what we do for God;* it is *who we are in God.* Many of us live unaware of our placement in God's Kingdom. The Word of God says that we are heirs through Christ, not slaves.[3] Our position in Christ gives us the right (through the blood of Christ), the authority, and the power to bring what is true in Heaven into the earthly realm.

The enemy cannot finish his structures of shame in our lives when we become aware of who we are in Christ. The enemy needs our permission to build those towers; every brick can only be laid by our agreement with him over our identity. The accuser will always bring up our past to get us out of our rightful place. In the story of Job, Satan spoke accusations through Job's friends. This tactic keeps us from fulfilling our destiny, which God planned out before the fall with the fall of man in mind. Thankfully God's power is stronger than any accusations or shame that has been sent your way, and He wants to remove the things in your life that are weakening you.

God is intentional, and He created you for a unique purpose. In Him, and through His power, you can fulfill that purpose and destiny regardless of any weakness. In Christ, shortcomings become opportunities for you to witness God's *power.* They become a front-row seat to see God's *capability.* Today, as you reflect on your position in Christ and His ability to move through you powerfully, let's clear out the enemy's stockpile of condemning stones and chastising mortar. May you be rid of his lies once and for all! Choose today to surrender that to the Lord. Greater surrender is required to clear the way to this opening of immeasurable power and might.

REFLECTION

In what area of my life do I need God's power (growing in faith, emotional strength in times of difficulty, increasing hope, financial provision, direction for the future, wisdom, healing)?

PRAYER

Father, heal me of my desperate striving for strength and ability! Help me to believe and rest in the truth that I am enough because I am Your child. I desire to fulfill my destiny! Show me what is in the way of me doing this, and give me the courage needed to surrender everything to You, trusting that You will become strong in all my weak areas. Show me how to access that power through Your Son today.

ACTIVATION

Prophesy over a specific area of your life that needs God's empowerment with this declaration: "I am a portal to God's mighty power!"

DAY 10: CULTIVATING THE GARDEN OF FAITH

Other seeds fell on rocky ground, where they did not have much soil, and immediately they sprang up, since they had no depth of soil, but when the sun rose they were scorched. And since they had no root, they withered away.
—Matthew 13:5–6, ESV—

INVITATION: SURRENDER THE GARDEN OF YOUR HEART TO THE MASTER GARDENER, LEAVING NO ROOM FOR UNBELIEF

When Jesus was talking about the sower and the seeds, He mentioned one set of seeds that fell among the hard ground that had no topsoil. This analogy represents a heart that has grown hard, pressed down, and impenetrable for any roots to cultivate. Because Jesus shared this with His followers, we can conclude that it is possible for a follower of Christ to develop a heart unable to grow and bear fruit. *Unbelief* is what causes this hardness in a believer's heart.

The Greek word for unbelief is *apistia,* which means faithlessness, disbelief, unfaithfulness, and disobedience. It comes from the root word *apistos,* which means unfaithful (not to be trusted), unbelieving, skeptical, and without trust in God.[1] Unbelief leads to spiritual blindness or a heart that cannot perceive the things of the Spirit. We can believe that Jesus was raised from the dead, accept Him as our Lord, and trust He is coming soon, but at the same time, we can have unbelief in Him as a *healer.* Unbelief begins to operate, eventually leading to spiritual blindness. That spiritual blindness will prevent us from experiencing His healing in the future unless we take steps to stop it in its tracks.

God says that all things are possible for those who believe, so in the same way, the person who operates under the influence of unbelief will never see the possibility God has provided for them. Jesus told us to ask anything in His name, and He will give it to us.[2] We wouldn't ask for healing if we were under the influence of unbelief in God as a healer, just like we wouldn't go to the doctor if we didn't believe the doctor would help us. Unbelief can cause us to miss out on the fulfillment of God's promises. From a faith perspective, unbelief is simply a resistance to the truth or distrust.

We must carefully understand the difference between unbelief and doubt, for they differ. Doubt is not the *resistance* to the truth but a *questioning* of the truth. We have to believe something first for doubt to creep in, which is a common struggle for every believer. Doubt can be beneficial because it alerts us to a problem of trust. Like a gas gauge in a car, it prompts us to fill ourselves up with faith by questioning and responding to that part of us that questions God's Word. Job brought his doubts to the Lord and didn't hold back, and this honesty propelled him into the presence of God. The critical thing to remember is that doubt can lead to unbelief unless we learn to take those things to Christ and stand on the Word of God, regardless of what we see going on around us.

Three things lead a believer into unbelief. The first is a hardened heart, or a heart that is immovable. Paul defined this as someone who, through willful ignorance, alienates themselves from God.[3] In other words, a hardened heart is like a branch that is severing itself from the tree. There is also a warning to us in Scripture that unbelief hides in plain sight, leading us astray and unresponsive to God.[4] That is why it becomes vital for us to guard the affections of our hearts.

The second thing that can lead us into unbelief is forgetting what God has done. There is this gravitational pull operating in the world called *forgetfulness* that can pull us away from faith and trust into skepticism. In the book of Job, Bildad mentioned that forgetting God withers our hope: *"Blossoming flowers look great before they're cut or picked, but without soil or water they wither more quickly than grass. That's what happens to all who forget God—all their hopes come to nothing"* (Job 8:12–13, MSG). Losing our memory about God is a common danger and does not require any effort to forget who we are and whose we are. Therefore, to protect ourselves from forgetting, we need to keep His ways in remembrance.

Finally, the third thing that can drive us into unbelief is an uncultivated thought life. Spiritual blindness is intricately connected to strongholds of the mind. As Paul told the believers in Corinth, it is a trick of the enemy to keep the light out: *"In their case the god of this world has blinded the minds of the unbelievers, to keep them from seeing the light of the gospel of the glory of Christ, who is the image of God"* (2 Corinthians 4:4, ESV).

Praise the Lord for the Holy Spirit, who gives us the power to overcome unbelief! He softens the soil of our hearts and plants the truth of His Word in each of us. God designed us to live in a realm of possibility with Christ. Believing that your Father is both willing and able to do the impossible today is what sets you apart from a world of unbelievers. According to Jesus, *"If you can believe, all things are possible"* (Mark 9:23, ESV). Belief says that God can do something better than you could ever ask, think, or imagine. And when you open your heart to trust Him more, those rocks of doubt and unbelief will get yanked out of your soul!

REFLECTION

There are four ways to protect yourself against unbelief:

1. Knowing God's will: *"So faith comes from hearing, and hearing through the word of Christ"* (Romans 10:17, ESV).
2. Rejecting fear: *"Don't be pulled in different directions or worried about a thing. Be saturated in prayer throughout each day, offering your faith-filled requests before God with overflowing gratitude"* (Philippians 4:6, TPT).
3. Believing in God's love: *"We have come into an intimate experience with God's love, and we trust in the love he has for us. God is love! Those who are living in love are living in God, and God lives through them"* (1 John 4:16, TPT).
4. Remembering your history with God: *"His unforgettable works of surpassing wonder reveal his grace and tender mercy"* (Psalm 111:4, TPT).

Which of these four areas is the Lord asking for more of my cooperation?

PRAYER

Holy Spirit, soften my heart today. Remove the stones of doubt and the hard soil of unbelief. Guide me into all truth, and lead me to an open space of all things possible in Christ.

ACTIVATION

Take the first step toward one of these four ways God puts on your heart. Commit yourself to checking in with God from time to time, making sure that you are on the right track. Cultivating the garden of your heart takes time and persistence. Don't let fear overwhelm you. Don't make it complicated. Just take the next step.

DAY 11: CARRY YOUR CROSS

If anyone would come after me,
let him deny himself and take up
his cross and follow me.
—Matthew 16:24, ESV—

INVITATION: SURRENDER YOUR WILL TO CARRY HIS WILL

Pain is disorienting and heavy. The length of our suffering through painful seasons can be varied, but it often feels like it's taking longer than it should. For Job, it felt like the resolution was taking too long, and we can see his struggle in the waiting period between the problem and the Lord's vindication. To make matters worse, some insensitive comforters began to offer suggestions. In the middle of our pain, we will encounter people who want to fix our problem, most of whom have good intentions. We live at a time when most people go out of their way to *avoid* pain, and so there are not a lot of sympathetic comforters around to empower us through the struggle. Unfortunately, our pain can sometimes attract heartless comforters; because they are uncomfortable with our hurt, they try their best to alleviate the suffering and take the discomfort away.

One of the familiar platitudes used today by insensitive comforters is related to the Scripture above. These well-meaning believers will tell you that what you are going through is *your cross to bear*. This statement lacks both compassion and understanding. While the Lord wants to teach us how to let go of taking the easy way out of pain, He doesn't want that pain to develop into a *lifestyle*. The truth is that the road God has us on will have many rugged valleys where our faith gets tested and our hearts get transformed. We have no idea how long we will be in the valley, and sometimes, we try to climb out of it on our own.

Amidst a period of suffering, it is also common for us to feel the urge to avoid personal growth. Avoidance of progressing with the Lord through hardship has two different options. The first is accepting the season of pain as a *lifestyle*, living on only the hope of *surviving*. There are times when the Lord will give us strategies to cope with the grief we are feeling or the pain that we are experiencing, but these are not meant to be persistent patterns in our lives. An example of this in the Bible is the Israelites, who refused to take the promised land and ended up in the wilderness for forty years. They did not grab hold of God's promise and provision in the desert, and therefore, they had no faith to stand on when they saw giants in the land God promised them. The waiting period we go through is meant to train us for *conquering*, but that will only happen when we take God at His Word. Israel's goal was self-preservation, which means they allowed fear to drive them out of their promised land.

The second option many choose during a wilderness season is trying to escape the waiting by rushing God's timing. The Israelites wanted to return to Egypt because they wanted to escape, trusting God to provide for their needs. Another example of this comes from the story of Abraham when his wife, Sarah, offered Abraham a way to speed up God's promise of a child. The problem was that God's promise included *Sarah*, not Hagar. This man-made solution was not a solution at all and instead caused unnecessary warfare. Looking for ways to speed up the developmental process always leads to trouble, and this is because the emotion leading the way, in this case, is pride, which manages our lives through self-promotion. Pride says to God, "I've got this." It can cause unnecessary heartache and pain, which God doesn't want us to experience. The better way to handle the waiting period in a season of suffering is to *surrender*. Yes, it is that simple, yet it can also be highly challenging. There are three basic steps we must take to *wait well*, with a heart submitted to God's ways. The first step is accepting this season of suffering as a *season* and not a lifestyle. An example of someone who did this was the story of Joseph, whose cooperation with God in the pit led him through pain and into a lifestyle of redemption.

The second step is looking for God's promises and provision in the wilderness. God takes care of us like He took care of Israel in the desert, but we have a responsibility to accept and receive what He is providing. We can see this in the life of Caleb, who kept his mind on what God had revealed to Israel in the desert, allowing God to develop his faith and believing he could take out those giants with God's help.

The final step is accepting your identity as God's warrior and training for when to take ground. An example of this in Scripture is Joshua, who fought his first battle at Jericho by obeying God's instructions to march around the city walls for a week, ending the march with trumpet blasts and shouting. We were made to take spiritual ground, and it is the Lord Jesus Christ who empowers us to conquer our promised land. The cross of Christ is where Jesus demonstrated His love for us and God. And we are told to follow His example. The purpose of carrying our cross isn't some platitude given by Jesus, for He doesn't use Band-Aids to fix our suffering. The goal is to show others what love *looks like*. No matter what flood rises against a child of God, there is a rock named Jesus, whom they can stand upon. Our life has not become easy; instead, we have allowed the King of the

Universe to display His strength through us in the waiting. Remember that whatever God calls you to do, He also provides grace to accomplish it, making it possible for you to do these two things:

1. Lay your desire to control your life down, choosing to love Him and others over your freedom. Pride and self-promotion must go!
2. Lay your coping mechanisms down, choosing trust in God over your fear. Anxiety and self-preservation must go!

By taking up your cross, you receive God in exchange. Surrendering your will may seem like a forfeit, but that is where your victory begins.

REFLECTION

What is God asking me to lay down and surrender (my will, fears, or shame)?

Ask God to reveal what He is giving you in exchange.

PRAYER

God, I want to follow Jesus, but I'm struggling to lay down some things in the season of waiting. Please help me to choose love over freedom and trust over fear.

ACTIVATION

In whatever God has asked you to surrender, picture yourself laying it down in front of the cross. Then ask Jesus to reveal what He wants to give you in exchange, and receive it by faith. As you walk in surrender, make this declaration from Psalm 23:4 over your life: *"Even when Your path takes me through the valley, fear and pride will never conquer me, for You already have! I surrender it all to You, Lord!"* (TPT).

DAY 12: EYES OF HOPE

Now I want you to know, believers, that what has happened to me [this imprisonment that was meant to stop me] has actually served to advance [the spread of] the good news [regarding salvation].
—Philippians 1:12, AMP—

INVITATION: SURRENDER YOUR EYESIGHT AND RECEIVE GOD'S EYES FOR THE TRIALS YOU FACE

Obedience to God attracts opposition. Satan's list of retaliation techniques to pull God's people off the course of their destiny is exhaustive. If you are ever wondering what you are called to do in this life, study the places where you are encountering the most resistance. Satan is a jerk, plain and simple. There should be no doubt that we have an adversary. However, it is our responsibility to consider this truth that all of Heaven is on our team when we are following the call of Christ in our lives. Can you feel the freedom of becoming partners with the Kingdom of Heaven? More are for us than those against us, despite what that warped mirror the devil holds up says.

The enemy's primary goal in your life is to convince you that he is stronger and that you should give up. Sometimes, things come at us right and left, exposing our vulnerable state. His strategy is to wear down the saints.[1] If Satan can rattle us enough, we could end up walking away from the high calling that Christ called us to before time began. We must look through another mirror, a heavenly lens, for Jesus has beckoned His followers to *"feast on all the treasures of the heavenly realm and fill our thoughts with heavenly realities, and not with the distractions of the natural realm"* (Colossians 3:2, TPT). Looking through Heaven's perspective will save us from hellish strategies dispatched to thwart our destinies.

What Hell had meant to break the church failed big time in the New Testament. The enemy intended to block the gospel from going any further, but those strategies backfired and became an instrument for the gospel. And that is how we can become confident that every impossible-seeming situation allows God to reveal His goodness to us. If you are facing an impossible circumstance, get ready to watch the Lord build a bridge around it, carve a tunnel under it, or walk with you through the fire.

Your pain has a purpose; it is your step stool to advance the Kingdom. To use this advantage, we must be willing to look through the heavenly reality and react differently than the world does. As the world continues to build its foundations on sandy shores, we need to build on our foundation on Christ, who is strong enough to withstand any storm in life. We have the advantage here because of our placement in Christ.

Life, especially for believers, is not free of problems. As you can see with Job and the apostle Paul, bad things happen to good people. Because of this promise of adversity, we need to anchor our souls in Christ. We must place in front of our eyes the good news and look through our situations with the advantage of being a son or daughter of God. Scripture tells us that *"every detail of our lives is continually woven together to fit into God's perfect plan of bringing good into our lives, for we are his lovers who have been called to fulfill his designed purpose"* (Romans 8:28, TPT).

The challenging circumstances we find ourselves in do not have to look good at the moment to be good in the end! It did not look good when Israel was stuck between the Red Sea and Pharaoh's army. It did not look good for Elijah when Jezebel was pursuing him. It did not look good for Lazarus when he died, either. At that moment on Calvary, Jesus on that cross did not look good. It did not look good for His followers either, but He rose from the dead and brought with Him the spoils of the enemy, which is your *good* news! Your situation may look ruined now, but God wants you to see how He is making it new—and more beautiful than before.

REFLECTION

The comfort, grace, and hope that I need to get through this hardship is with me. His name is Jesus.

Where can I see Him in my life right now?

What would bring Him into greater focus?

PRAYER

Father, I need a new pair of spiritual glasses today. I need a new revelation from You about my hardships. I agree with Your Word that You have given me eternal comfort and good hope through the grace provided by Your Son, Jesus. Now, I ask for Your comfort to embrace my heart and establish me in every good work and word.

ACTIVATION

As you turn your gaze upon Jesus, make this declaration over yourself: "God has given me eyes to see Jesus in my hardships! I am fixing my eyes on Him today!"

DAY 13: SPIRIT, LEAD ME

Praise the Lord, my soul;
all my inmost being, praise his holy name.
—Psalm 103:1, NIV—

INVITATION: SURRENDER YOUR EMOTIONS TO GOD AND BECOME SPIRIT-LED

There is a time when the pit feels too deep to climb out of. And there is a pressure, from both the outside and the inside, to let our soul sit in the driver's seat, determining what direction we go. This pressure can leave us feeling overwhelmed by unruly thoughts and feelings. We see Job struggle with those pressures, wrestling with his feelings and what he knows to be true about God. All pain can bring a sense of powerlessness, and those parts of you that have been permitted to lead you will dig their heels in even more to keep their seated position. They think they know the best way to protect you from pain, and if left to their own devices, they will keep you from growing up in Christ.[1]

There are parts of us that aim to build up walls of protection, but there are also parts of us that stay under our radar. Some parts are so hurt, and they need to be held and loved by the Lord to find healing. There is mismanagement that can take place when we try to do all of these things on our own, without God. He longs to come alongside us, helping us learn how to go from soul-driven to spirit-led. He yearns to be your *only* protection, leading you into a place of wholeness.

There are several ways the Bible describes being *soul-driven*. Paul described a soul being driven by a carnal mind, and he said that this carnality is at war with God.[2] The word carnal refers to the physical feelings, wants, and desires of the body. To be carnally minded means to feed that which will satisfy the physical body and the soul. This carnality can lead people into addictive behaviors and unhealthy lifestyles that gratify themselves but do not serve God or others. Another word used to describe this is the *flesh*. The word flesh represents all that is natural, earthly, and human. It includes what we can experience with our physical senses. The flesh will deny access to the Spirit of God, which is why the Lord told us to die to our flesh. The apostle Paul said, *"If you live according to the flesh you will die; but if by the Spirit you put to death the deeds of the body, you will live"* (Romans 8:13, NKJV). If we feed our flesh, allowing that to drive our actions, that will lead us down the path of destruction. However, if we feed our spirit, permitting God's Spirit to lead us, that will take us to life in Christ.

There are two divisions of your soul that need the ministry of Jesus to help keep you on the path of life. The first division is the part of your soul trying to *protect you,* led by a specific emotion. Fear is one example of a *protector*. If someone has experienced pain, fear will kick in to protect them from getting hurt again. We see this happen often in relationships; our protector emotion will get us to avoid people because it's trying to protect us from getting hurt again.

Another example of an emotion trying to protect you is anger. Anger is typically linked with powerlessness. It is trying to keep things in order so you don't feel out of control. These parts are doing their best, but they do not have what it takes to make you whole or keep you on the path of life. They need to be acknowledged by you, have boundaries put in place, and be brought to Jesus so that He can remain near and help you manage these unruly parts.

Another division of your soul that needs ministry is the part of you that has been lost. These are also known as your *exiles*. They were most likely banished by your *protectors* who want to protect you from memories that caused pain. These parts are longing to feel the comfort of Christ, and they will usually come out of hiding when the Lord knows you are ready to give them to His Lordship. An example of this would be memories of rejection. Say there is a hurt part of you that didn't feel seen or loved as a child. That part needs the healing of Jesus. When this part of you receives healing (over time), and the protectors learn to step back, letting the Spirit of God lead the way, you will find yourself under new, life-producing management.

A spirit-led person is not perfect but *honest* because they cooperate with God despite their feelings. For the spirit isn't focused on feelings or earthly desires. It isn't centered on pleasing the self. Instead, it is driven to please the Lord and others. This part becomes most active when our souls rest. When we are sleeping, when we are taking a day of physical rest from the toils of life, and when we take moments to delight ourselves in the Lord, we are feeding our spirit.

The Lord also admonishes us to give thanks in every situation because when we do that, we feed our spirit, allowing the surge of God's strength and power to flow through us. Our flesh would have us complain, but the Spirit of God within us sets our hearts to lead the way with gratitude. Part of learning how to let God's Spirit lead you is understanding how to teach your soul to trust God in the process you are in. We can learn to be spirit-led by following these three things with Jesus:

1. Stay curious about your soul. Jesus wants us to catch inferior thoughts that hinder our relationship with Him, and He will teach us how to do this in a way that doesn't cause further damage.
2. You have permission to ask parts of your soul to step back. Setting them back doesn't mean that they are healed; it only means that you are still in the driver's seat, not allowing a backseat driver to control where you are going.
3. Ask Jesus to be near each part of you. Healing comes in waves and layers. Be patient with yourself as you learn how to let Jesus minister to your soul. This step will look different for each person. Jesus always comes near to restore. His hands always redeems that which has been lost. We are no longer orphans but sons and daughters of a loving Father.

REFLECTION

What protector is in the driver's seat of my soul? (It can be helpful to name an emotion attached to this part, like fear, anger, sadness, or pride.)

What boundaries do I need to put around that part of me? (Do you need it to take a step back, or are you ready to invite Jesus to be near?)

PRAYER

Holy Spirit, please lead the way in my life. I am ready for the redemptive blood of Christ to come into my inward parts and bring healing, restoration, and order. Show me how to submit to Your will and way as I trust even more of myself to You.

ACTIVATION

Declare this Scripture out loud, moving your soul closer to Jesus: *"Praise the Lord, my soul; all my inmost being, praise His holy name! Praise the Lord, my soul, and forget not all His benefits– who forgives all of my sins and heals all of my diseases, who redeems my life from the pit and crowns me with love and compassion, who will satisfy my desires with good things so that my youth may be renewed like the eagle's!"* (Psalm 103:1–5, NIV).

DAY 14: COMFORT THROUGH COMPASSION

He always comes alongside us to comfort us in every suffering so that we can come alongside those who are in any painful trial. We can bring them this same comfort that God has poured out upon us."
—2 Corinthians 1:4, TPT—

INVITATION: SURRENDER YOUR EARTHLY COMFORT TO MOVE WITH COMPASSION TOWARD YOURSELF AND OTHERS

Job eventually found himself surrounded by friends who were clueless in the area of comfort. He emphasized that they whitewashed the truth with lies and were a bunch of worthless physicians.[1] Job begged them to keep silent. If there were ever someone who understands how it feels to have their honor smeared, it would be Job. Zophar, Eliphaz, and Bildad took turns accusing him of wrongdoing and throwing mud on his character. Unyielding to these many insults and injuries, Job refused to relent in his confidence of integrity. The three stooges continued to press him in on all sides by using his confidence as evidence of arrogance. Job couldn't say anything right. He was doomed if he did and doomed if he did not.

Whether we would like to admit it or not, we, too, can injure and maim our own friends and family members if we do not carefully guard our hearts and tongues in our response to their suffering. We often try to explain the reason for suffering, even when the cause is unknown, because our humanity dislikes mysteries and desires to see every situation explained and corrected. It was why the fruit from the knowledge of good and evil looked so tempting to Eve. Unfortunately, this side of Heaven contains many mysteries and paradoxes without visible explanation. In the book of Job, nobody on earth knew what had taken place in the heavenly courtroom between the Lord and Satan. Job's friends were trying to make sense of their friend's suffering, and because of that, they wounded their friend instead of comforting him.

What Job's friends were missing was *compassion*. They cut him deeply when they should have loved him deeply. And we could make the same error with our loved ones if we choose explanation over comfort. The Holy Spirit can guide us into being a comforter like Jesus, helping us show compassion and love. But to do this, we must agree to become His pupils, listening to His voice for what to say and how to pray. The light of the world that Jesus talked about in the Gospels can shine through our compassion and love.[2]

To follow in Jesus's footsteps, let us examine how He approached people in pain. In the Gospel of John, Jesus noticed a man who was born blind. He *noticed* him. That is the first step we must take in comforting others like Jesus. We must make enough margin in our lives to see those needing a touch from Him. How do the disciples react? They must have taken advice on comforting from Bildad, Zophar, and Eliphaz! They were poking around for reasons why this man was born blind. They asked if it was the blind man's or his parent's fault. But immediately after they responded out of ignorance,

Jesus swooped in with His love and compassion and said, *"Neither. It happened to him so that you could watch him experience God's miracle"* (John 9:3, TPT). One could imagine such an answer coming as a shock to the disciples and others around. Jesus's response was dripping with compassion. He was training His disciples and us to listen when God instructs us to move in situations with love and tenderness.

We cannot miss His voice; we must tune in with a righteous desire to comfort those who are mourning and in pain. We must overcome this uncomfortable feeling when we do not have the answers. Jesus lived in uncomfortable situations, so does following Him mean that we will have to get uncomfortable? Indeed, the life of a disciple is not a cakewalk. Following Jesus means we sit in the grit and lean in, waiting to hear the promise that is attached to the problems our loved ones and strangers are facing.

Your mission field is *where you are*. If you let the Holy Spirit open your eyes, He will guide you in becoming a minister of hope to everyone who crosses your path. When we become a vessel of compassion, our eyes suddenly see where our help is needed. All at once, you will see a neighbor who needs encouragement, a cashier who needs prayer for healing, and a kid who needs a prophetic word spoken over their situation. You could see a stranger stranded and needing assistance or an elderly relative who needs someone to talk to. Those things are ministry. We do not need fancy titles to lead in compassion. Look at what God has given you and start there!

REFLECTION

Who needs my comfort today?

How is the Lord leading me to bring comfort to that person?

PRAYER

Lord, I need You to teach me how to operate compassionately like Jesus in uncomfortable situations. Please unlock that ability within me to comfort those around me. Please show me what to do. When it becomes hard for me and uncomfortable, please strengthen my courage to sit in pain with people and love them without an explanation. Thank You for all the comfort You've given me. Now, make me into a vessel that pours Your comfort into others.

ACTIVATION

Be alert for someone the Lord wants to comfort through you today. Move with His compassion and minister His love to them in whatever way He shows you.

WEEK 3: IDENTITY

There I will give her her vineyards and make the Valley of Achor [troubling] to be for her a door of hope and expectation.
—Hosea 2:15, AMPC—

INVITATION: EMBRACE YOUR GOD-GIVEN IDENTITY WHILE ALSO REMEMBERING HIS IDENTITY

Identity shapes how we see everything, so it is imperative to obtain our view of God and ourselves through the Word of God. He is taking us on a journey of continuous discovery. If we want to know God more intimately, we must remove Him from our man-made religious parameters while still viewing everything through the lens of Scripture. The *wilderness season* is the place where God reveals Himself the most. However, there is a battle over what God has said about Himself. The Lord wants to take you from *knowing* Him to *understanding* Him. Knowing is a surface-level revelation of God's nature and ways, but we must seek God more sincerely. There is an invitation in the wilderness season to understand Him in a way only discovered through personally encountering His presence.

When facing an illness without a cure in my life, the warfare revealed God as Jehovah Rapha, the God who heals. When my husband's job was on the line, the fight displayed God as Jehovah Jireh, the God who provides. When I started experiencing regular panic attacks, the battle brought me to God as Jehovah Shalom, the God of peace. We win the identity battle by keeping the *truth* about God above all speculation. God's eternal truth has supreme authority over all other ideologies.

The pessimistic mindset is ingrained into our human nature, focusing on problems while dressing itself up to appear reasonable or sensible. We must think with a Kingdom mindset that sees the truth while responding to God's voice. Every obstacle is an assigned time for discovering a new part of God's identity. We must learn to stand against the opposition and confess God's identity over our circumstances. This method is something referred to by many as *moving in the opposite spirit*. David used this tactic when encountering resistance; he fought many inward battles with God's name! In Psalm 23, David referred to God as "Jehovah Raah," which means *the Lord is my Shepherd*. God wants to reveal Himself to you as He did for David because He desires close fellowship.

This week, we will concentrate on what the Bible says about God's nature. The Lord will use this time to shape your identity so that you will refuse any counterfeits. You will learn how to practice raising your expectations of God while waiting for the fulfillment of a promise, which will open up the door of hope in your life.

In the following letter, the Father wants to remind you who He is for you and your placement in His heart. How He sees you will transform your life, but it will require a renewal of your mind. The Father will only be content once you are free, whole, clear, and clean. It's time to raise your expectations of yourself and God to a new level. Someday, looking back at this part of your life, you will say, "This is my history —and this is who God was for me."

Beloved,

Every situation in your life is an opportunity to deepen your friendship with Me. Did you know that My identity in your heart is the most significant perception of your life? For it shapes how you will come to Me, which then directs your steps forward. My dear one, no matter what you face, you can always anticipate discovering My identity. Instead of uncertainty, I will cause you to encounter a rising confidence in My love for you. Remember, I am making you into My image and My likeness.

I am looking forward to you learning My language of love toward you. I need you to remember that the old you is dead; it died with Jesus on the cross. When He died, you died! And when He came to life, a new you was resurrected with Him! So, we aren't going to focus on what's dead in you but on what Jesus regenerated in you. The seed of My love is already in your life, which is why the warfare has been intense. The enemy is out to exploit any ignorance of My identity, and this makes your oneness with Jesus your most significant advantage on this journey. As the certainty of My promises becomes your greater reality, the language of your prayers will change. You will know what questions to ask. You will discover how to shape your prayers to hit their target of My purpose consistently.

I love telling you what I want to do in you, for you, through you, and around you. So, come and walk with Me in My Kingdom. The Kingdom is now your everyday habitat. And My Son, Jesus, wants to welcome you to the place where all things are possible through Him. The vocabulary you will use here is faith and expectation. Your expectation will grow because your trust in Me is beginning to expand. I am unchanging, which means I'm predictable. You can count on My faithfulness.

You are on this unique pilgrimage to being fully persuaded of My love for you. Will you begin to raise your expectations of My goodness in your life? Will you begin to practice My identity in yourself? Trust will empower your heart to believe by overturning disempowered languages. I will change your internal atmosphere from toxic cynicism to joyful declaration. Will you practice this joyous submission with Me? Leave worldly thinking behind. You are on your way to becoming sure of the Kingdom you belong to. Your language about yourself and Me is transforming, for you are learning the language of My promise. Remember, I am fully committed to you, and I am not going anywhere. Receive My acceptance as your gift, and come with Me.

Love,
Your Abba Father

Additional Reading Option: Job Chapters 15–21

DAY 15: YOU ARE HIS WITNESS

But you will receive power and ability
when the Holy Spirit comes upon you; and you
will be My witnesses [to tell people about Me]
both in Jerusalem and in all Judea, and Samaria,
and even to the ends of the earth.
—Acts 1:8, AMP—

INVITATION: IDENTIFY YOURSELF AS GOD'S WITNESS

The story of Job is structured in the form of a courtroom. There were three witnesses (proven later to be false) building their case against Job, finding him guilty of punishment. However, there was an even greater trial that took place in a heavenly courtroom. Satan slandered God's name and accused Him of acquiring relationships with people like Job through bribery. He was trying to prove that there was no authentic love between God and man. Not much has changed, for a great trial is underway between the powers of evil and the perfect Lord of all things good.

Hidden from sight, in the unseen realm, there are spiritual beings whose intent is to warp the truth, deceiving humans about God's love, which is demonstrated to us through Jesus. There are moments when the truth appears to be prevailing, but more often than not, the days when it is treated as a myth or a legend are more common. The trial over truth in this hour is still underway; Satan is bringing forth his witnesses who are willing to slander the name of Jesus. Where are God's witnesses on earth? Where are those summoned to deliver a testimony of eternal truth? We are the ones God calls in this great trial of the ages to stand forward as witnesses for Christ!

Knowing the truth about Jesus and His love for mankind comes from reading the Word of God with an open heart. Corrupted hearts often misinterpret the Word's message. Thankfully we receive truth from more than words, for God's Spirit is the one who helps us interpret its authentic message. We must align our hearts and minds to what has been written and follow the Spirit of the Lord to learn its meaning. Christ's love is revealed through His Word, which propels us to become His willing witnesses, dwelling in God's truth and nothing but the truth. We must proclaim a good confession in the thick of untruths, regardless of the outcome.

God has equipped us with His power to be Christ's witnesses. Everything that we need has already been deposited in our heavenly account,[1] including wisdom and revelation.[2] God's resources for you to be His witness are never exhausted because He can do exceedingly and abundantly above all that you can ask or think, and He has more strength to give to you day to day when you become a weary witness. When you cannot find the words, the Holy Spirit will draw from the well of God's Word living inside your heart, and He will give you the correct response and help you speak the truth when it needs to be communicated.

There is a stark contrast between telling a secondhand spiritual experience and a firsthand personal testing and trying of God's promises in His Word. You are called to be His *personal* witness and testify what you have seen of God and felt for yourself. How have you tasted and seen God's goodness in your pain? Your trials and deliverances are most beneficial to those who are searching for hope. Even when the resolution of your hardship encounters delay, Christ upholds and supports your life in a way that others must hear. When someone is in pain and seeking truth, it's important to share God's faithfulness and not remain silent in the face of slander. Deception gives people a dead end, but your testing of the Scriptures and personal account of Christ releases people to keep fighting the good fight of faith. You have a responsibility to provide options to the hurting and the misled, options they couldn't see before you gave your personal witness.

The Hebrew word *ʿēḏûṯ* is found in the Old Testament and translated as the words "witness" and "testimony." The general meaning of the root word for *ʿēḏûṯ* is to "return" or to "do again."[3] When we testify of what God has done in our lives, the same power is released. This power of giving testimony is why many Messianic rabbis will connect a person who has a specific type of illness with a person who has been healed of that same illness. The person who has been healed testifies to the one in need, opening the door for them to experience Christ's healing.[4]

The ancient pictographs of the root word for "testimony" are pictures of an eye and a door. Your testimony allows others to see Jesus, who is the doorway of our faith, and encourages them to walk by faith. A person who bears witness to healing can testify that "Jesus still heals" is true. They can then testify about this knowledge to others, and in this way, the others will know it as well. How can you bring testimony to the people in your life of who Jesus is and what He has done for you? Recall how God has proved His love for you, and be ready to share. Your personal testimony is the gospel of Christ that releases the power of God to do it again in other people's lives.

What keeps us ready as Christ's witnesses is an earnest prayer life. Preserving our connection with God's Spirit, the source of truth, keeps us in a place of empowerment, where we can focus on what He sees instead of the lies and distractions from the deceiver. And we bring glory to God through His power of truth in us like that of Gideon, who had his small army carry empty jars with torches inside to the enemy's territory with no physical weapons.[5] We have been given a prophetic message of power and grace to conquer, and our testimonies become someone else's empowerment to overcome. Like that small army, we sound the trumpet by proclaiming how the Word of the Lord has been steadfast in our lives. The clay jars in the story of Gideon represent each of us, for we are clay jars, broken so that Christ, the burning light of glory within us, can display His light of truth. May God's glorious truth be revealed in us and through us, His witnesses in the earth.

REFLECTION

What testimonies do I carry of Christ's truth and faithfulness? (These can be specific instances of where God revealed Himself to you in a unique way or a testimony of transformation or healing.)

PRAYER

Jesus, help me to be Your witness. Reveal the testimonies of Yourself that I carry, and remind me of the empowerment to be Your witness today.

ACTIVATION

You are empowered by the Holy Spirit to be a witness of Christ! Who does God want you to witness to? Is there someone who needs to hear how God showed up in your life when you needed Him? Keep it simple; you don't have to share the whole gospel. Just step out in faith and share your personal testimony of what Christ has done in your life!

DAY 16: HE IS YOUR ROCK AND YOUR DEFENSE

He only is my rock and my salvation;
He is my defense; I shall not be greatly moved.
—Psalm 62:2, NKJV—

INVITATION: IDENTIFY GOD AS YOUR PLACE OF STABILITY AND SAFETY

Our world is experiencing a great shaking as the day of the Lord draws near. The purpose of the shaking is to expose hidden things, such as insecurities. Anything outside of Jesus Christ, our solid rock, will be shaken and fall away. Especially in the storms of life, we must place both our feet on an unshakable foundation. Hardships will always reveal where we have a wrong security in our hearts. It is truly one of the most uncomfortable feelings, and unless we invite the Holy Spirit into that exposure, it will move us into a place of shame. The Lord only exposes our insecurities with our redemption in mind, like in the story of Job. God also doesn't traffic us through humiliation or use punishment as a tool of control or manipulation in our lives.

Exposure is a sign of God's love and goodness. He knows that whenever we step outside of His fortress, we become prey for the adversary. It may sound like wisdom to our ears, but the thought, *I've got this, and I can handle this one on my own,* is a lie. God will always respect your choices, as poor as they may be, but His heart longs for you to run back to Him. The word used for security is defined as freedom from danger or injury.[1] Learning our security in Christ makes us feel safe, comforted, and secure. Any security we find outside of Christ is unstable ground. Examples of where we find this inferior security varies depending on the person and the season of life they are in. For some, it's relationships; for others, it's money. Some may find security in their position at their workplace or in their gifts. If we focus on that and build our life around those *good* things, we will build on a precarious bedrock. What keeps us there? There are three main hindrances to seeing God as a place of safety.

The first hindrance is hyperfocus on the opposition. One of the best examples is Peter, who took His eyes off Jesus and onto the storm. Fear is the emotion that drives us to *tolerate* a shakable foundation. Fear can become a lifestyle unless we fight it with God's Word. At a time when the wind is howling and the waves are crashing all around us, we can feel completely overwhelmed. At that point, we must run to the safety of our Savior and allow Him to fight what we cannot handle on our own. We must surrender to Jesus, giving up our fear and worry and throwing them to the cross. Mary is an example of a person unmoved by anything.[2] She prized the time with Jesus and gave her entire focus to His presence. Jesus ensured that nothing took her away from Him, even the worry and fear of her sister, Martha. There are some things we may need to give up or boundaries in relationships we need to put in place to get our feet back on the rock of Christ.

The second hindrance to seeing God as a place of safety is forgetting our personal history with Him. An example of this is how the Israelites walked through the wilderness. They did not rehearse their history of God's works and ways, and because of that, fear crept into their hearts. When they saw the giants in the land of promise, they saw them as bigger than God, even though the Lord had done incredible miracles and brought them out of bondage. They rehearsed their fears, complaints, and troubles instead of rehearsing the way God had led them across the Red Sea, drowning their enemies behind them, or how God fed them with Heaven's bread and provided water from a rock. They forgot how God had given them victory over the Amalekites, who had preyed upon their vulnerability. We must practice *thanksgiving* and *testifying* what God has done regularly. David is our example of someone who reminded himself of how God had been good to him. His remembrance built walls of protection in His relationship with God.

The final hindrance is self-sufficiency. Disguised as freedom, it will leave you open to attack. Independence *from* God happens when we look to ourselves for stability and security. We are incapable of defending and guarding ourselves without Christ. Self-preservation also has the capability of causing huge problems down the road, affecting future generations. Abraham and Sarah thought God needed their help with fulfilling His promise of a child to them. God's promise was not reserved for Abraham and *Hagar* but for Abraham and *Sarah*. Out of Sarah's insecurity came Ishmael, who became a thorn in Israel's side for thousands of years. The opposite example was Paul and Silas inside the prison walls, where they waited on God. They recognized their inability to get out of the mess they were in. They weren't praising God to get something from Him, but in authentic praise and enduring patience, God liberated them from their jail cell. We have to remember that He's the same liberating God!

In Psalm 62, David recognized his insufficiency to save himself, especially when faced with human oppressors. In the very first verse of the psalm, David announced to his soul where salvation is found. He claimed that his soul *waited in silence* for God alone, which means that David had ceased looking for something or someone else to save him. Secondly, David put his weary soul under submission to God. He refrained from protesting, complaining, or worrying. He set his heart on God, and like Mary, he would not be moved until his inner being was strengthened and secure in God alone.

We can put a name to whom David was calling his rock, salvation, and defense. The Lord Jesus Christ is our solid rock and our greatest defender. He will not be moved from the promises He has made, and He will not turn away from us because of His unending love and affection. We can place our trust in Jesus above everything else. His faithfulness is consistent, stable, fixed, constant, steady, loyal, dedicated, devout, reliable, dependable, solid, genuine, passionate, steadfast, unwavering, determined, and expected.

His faithfulness will not oscillate in a time of great shaking. Jesus is a rock that will not be moved through any age. Nothing is greater than Jesus Christ, and the winds and the waves still obey His voice. Not only is He a safe place, unshakable, but He is also the water that comes out of the rock. In waterless places in our lives, He is preserving us. His Spirit was poured out like water upon us, leading us and connecting us to the source of life.

Besides His faithfulness and preservation, Jesus is also our defender. In the story of Job, we see dialogue between several people; arguments and disputes occur between Job and his friends, everyone looking for something and someone to blame. His friends hurled many false accusations against Job, who was desperate for someone to speak up for him. Like Job, we may have current circumstances or past issues of accusation. Whether in the natural or the supernatural, we have accusers.

For us, today, we have a defender who speaks on our behalf, seeking justice for us in the courtroom of Heaven. Jesus is our defense attorney, and He is on our side. He will not put up with any lies spoken against us and has given us His righteousness in exchange for our filthy garments of self-righteousness. There is no one else who can bring justice to our lives. Jesus made us right before God. What a Savior, what a friend! We were guilty until He came to our defense, taking our punishment and making us clean before the Father.

Jesus removed the shackles of sin, death, and oppression. He proclaimed the year of grace, God's favor for man. So now, we must learn to cooperate with His generous grace, reminding ourselves that He paid a great price for our sake. We must not accept false accusations but remember to take insecure thoughts captive, commanding their obedience to the solid Word of God, Jesus Christ. We must learn to replace those inferior things with the superior truth of God's Word. Those promises and declarations over our lives are greater strongholds that can withstand the shaking in any storm.

Three ways to move into that stronghold of Christ are becoming intolerant to lies, placing boundaries upon your gates (of your heart and mind), and refusing inferior thoughts to have a place of influence. We also must remember the ways God has saved us in the past (our history), write them down, and recount them often. We must exchange our fear for His love and surrender any influence of self-sufficiency. Then, and only then, will we gain safety in a shaking world. When we make Jesus Christ our only hope, our greatest expectation, nothing will move us from Him.

REFLECTION

What lie have I been believing about Jesus being a rock and my defender?

In what way am I trying to defend myself?

Are both of my feet on Jesus, or am I finding other things that make me feel safe outside of Him?

PRAYER

Jesus, show me the truth! Remind me of our history together. I am giving up on trying to do this on my own. Please show me where there is any outside influence so that I can run away from that and back into Your loving arms!

ACTIVATION

It's important to declare trust in Jesus's identity as *your* defender in specific situations. Today, take time to picture what Jesus revealed to you in the reflection portion of today's devotional. How is Jesus defending you? What is He holding? What expression is on His face? Is there a word He is speaking to your heart? Let Him reveal His faithfulness to defend those He loves. He is fighting for you!

DAY 17: HE IS YOUR REAR GUARD

For you shall not go out in haste, and you shall not go in flight, for the LORD will go before you, and the God of Israel will be your rear guard.
—Isaiah 52:12, ESV—

INVITATION: IDENTIFY GOD AS YOUR REAR GUARD, ONE WHO PROTECTS YOU FROM YOUR ENEMIES AND YOUR PAST

The Lord Jesus Christ is calling you to follow Him. Just as He called Israel out of Egypt, Christ has called you out of bondage. God is faithful to us even after we cross the Red Sea, where He drowned our enemies, removing their authority. Like with Israel, God's presence goes with us and surrounds us day and night. The Israelites had a sign of His ongoing presence, a cloud by day and fire by night. The cloud by day covered them from the daily heat of the desert; the fire by night provided the light they needed to travel and warmth. The cloud and fire were a supernatural manifestation of His eternal promise to Israel. He promised to be with them, and so He was.

His love never turned away. The symbols of His loving presence revealed His nature as their protector, provider, refuge, strength, and safeguard. In the same way, God's Spirit is with each of us as our shield, fortress, hiding place, keeper, refuge, rock, shade, shelter, and stronghold. There is opposition to our progress forward. The enemy does not want us to take ground, and we are thrust into a war over dominion. Who will have authority in our hearts?

There are two ways the enemy tries to stop our progress: intimidation and manipulation. Intimidation is *plan A*, which is his blatant strategy. It is a Goliath in our territory[1] or a threat from Sennacherib's servant.[2] Fear is the main tactic the enemy uses to make you turn back and give up. The closer you get to walking on God's path, the more intense the warfare over your steps will be. Satan cannot forcibly take you back, so he aims to bully you to turn around.

If intimidation doesn't work, the devil will use manipulation—*plan B*. This tactic is subtle and not as easily detected. Staying connected to Jesus protects us against those subtle deceptions. Manipulation refers to repetitive tactics that undermine someone's well-being to exert power over them.[3] This form of control is like Delilah's strategy to get Samson to relinquish the secret of his strength and disobey God.[4] When the Philistines learned that intimidating Samson wouldn't work, they found a crack in his foundation—a desire for passion *outside* of God. The enemy knows your misalignment and seeks to exploit that weakness. His goal is to manipulate you into distrusting God. Like the snake in the garden, he wants to convince you that God is holding out on you. The temptation is to find nourishment, comfort, and transformation outside God's love.

There is also a lure to look back. When Lot's wife looked back at the destruction of Sodom and Gomorrah, it wasn't just a passing glance.[5] The Hebrew word for "look back" is *nāḇaṭ*, and it means to look intently at; by implication, to regard with pleasure, favor, or care, to consider, regard, and have respect for.[6] A desire, or a longing, was pulling Lot's wife back. And that same allurement is presented to us when God leads us away from destruction. In the prophetic book of Isaiah, the Lord warned us about looking back when He said, *"Remember not the former things, nor consider the day of old"* (Isaiah 43:18, ESV). When God talked about forgetting the past, He warned us not to allow our history to have the wrong influence over our future. Verse 19 says, *"Behold, I am doing a new thing; now it springs forth, do you not perceive it?"*

In the story of Job, he had trouble looking forward. His friends constantly brought up false accusations about how he lived in the past, a similar tactic that the enemy uses on us to keep us from moving forward. Christ has gone into our past and removed its sting. There may be some areas of your past that still need healing, but Jesus does not want you to remain stuck there. He wants to go into your history to redeem those memories. Jesus knows that if we keep looking behind us, we will not perceive the new thing God is doing. In Paul's letter to the Philippian church, he told them that to press on toward the goal of the call of Christ, he had to forget what lies behind and strain forward to what lies ahead.[7]

Job felt as if pleasing God by living according to His ways was his identity, so when the rug got pulled out from under him, he was confused. Identity confusion can happen even to those who know Christ. We must understand that God formed us with a unique purpose beyond what we can do *for* God. We must also see our lives in the light of eternity. We are not only living for this life! We are part of a Kingdom that will never pass away, and suffering does not have the authority to take us out of that calling. Our instructions are to seek the Kingdom of God above everything else, and the Kingdom lies in front of us, not behind us. Jesus warned us that *"No one who puts his hand to the plow and looks back is fit for the Kingdom of God"* (Luke 9:62, ESV). We cannot let pain and hardship distract us from looking ahead. We must keep our eyes fixed on Christ, who is our rear guard, and the King of the Universe.

Israel is an example of a nation that kept looking back. They began longing for Egypt, wishing they had never left. We often return to what is familiar and comfortable. Egypt was predictable because there was no trust involved as a *slave*. They were uncertain of God's intentions, even after He had displayed His might and power to set them free. That same human weakness runs through our veins. The temptation for Israel was to return to what was familiar. That temptation is why many people (not all) today lose their healing. There is a part of them that is scared of change and wants to live with what is predictable or familiar. The other temptation is to look back with a negative mindset, only seeing our path from one problem to the next. This negative view is not the mindset of the new man that Christ raised at your salvation; it is the old you who passed away on the cross with Christ. What Jesus killed, let it stay dead. When we make it a habit, we begin to doubt God's power and willingness to redeem.

The solution to these temptations is to *believe* and *trust* God's presence surrounding us. Not only are you surrounded by God, but He surrounds you with ministering angels. Jesus is the Lord of Angel Armies, and we are on the *winning* team. Psalm 46:11 says, *"The mighty Lord of Angel Armies is on our side!"* Jesus went ahead of us and won the victory so we don't have to fear what lies before us. There is comfort in knowing that the unknown is full of God's presence.

Besides being a mighty and vital force in front of us, Jesus is our rear guard, as He was the pillar of fire behind Israel, blocking the enemy from recapturing them. Jesus has our back in this fight against despair, hopelessness, and pain. As our defender, He is standing up against our accusers and speaking out against every false claim. With Jesus, we are taking ground, and there is no turning back. We are moving forward because Jesus in us won't back down. We can take the next step forward, trusting God's presence before and behind us.

REFLECTION

What is holding me back from moving forward (fear of the unknown, doubt that God will protect me from behind, shame about my past, or discouragement)?

What lie is behind that temptation to doubt God's will for me to reach the other side?

PRAYER

Thank You, Jesus, for going ahead of me and having my back. Reveal to my heart the truth that You want to replace those lies about my ability to follow You and move forward in my journey. Help my heart to trust You more as I wait for You to finish what You started in me.

ACTIVATION

Aren't you grateful that Jesus is on *your* side? Today, continue to take a stand against anything that would take you backward. As you submit to the Lord, make this declaration over your life: "I trust Jesus as my rear guard and refuse to go backward!"

DAY 18: HE IS YOUR LOVING FATHER

Look with wonder at the depth of the Father's love that he has lavished on us! He has called us and made us his very own beloved children.
—1 John 3:1, TPT—

INVITATION: IDENTIFY GOD AS YOUR LOVING FATHER

A Loving Father

Picture a sweet and precious ten-month-old girl named Annabelle teetering on the edge of an old green leather couch, standing tall and proud, making all kinds of noises and giggles. Her bare belly exposed because of the spaghetti she had played with earlier that evening prompted an immediate washing of her shirt before the stain set. Her cheeks still bear the stain of tomato sauce she had used as face paint at dinner. Suddenly, her dad walks into the room from the hallway, and Annabelle notices him approaching her, barely able to contain her glee. He kneels to her level, motioning with his arms that he wants her to come to him. Annabelle lets go of the couch and takes three wobbly steps toward her dad. Drool is hanging down her mouth, dripping onto her belly, and teeth peek out from behind her massive grin. She falls and crawls as fast as she can toward her dad. When she reaches him, he scoops her up into his arms and kisses her on both cheeks, holding her face close to his. He says to her over and over, "I love you, Annabelle! Daddy loves you!"

~

The scene described above is a snapshot of an interaction between a loving father and his precious child, the same way your heavenly Father interacts with you, His beloved child. Unfortunately, we can develop a distorted view of the Father through bad experiences with our earthly fathers or other father figures. There may also be circumstances that have stirred up unresolved conflict between faith and doubt in the Father's goodness. It's time to address those lies that have formed friction in your relationship with your loving Father.

We address lies by speaking the truth that our loving Father will never leave us. He cannot abandon or reject us because of the promises of unyielding love He has made over us. Even if we walk away, He follows us. For it says in Psalm 139:5, *"You hem me in, behind and before, and lay your hand upon me"* (ESV). The love of our Father also restrains Him from punishing us. Even when we fall like Annabelle, there is no shame in God's love, and He doesn't hold your past against you. Jesus took on God's wrath, our punishment, upon Himself at the cross. He carried both sin and its consequence of shame away forever! God's grace and mercy do not imply that He has lowered His standards; instead, they reveal He will never allow our imperfections to separate us from His love.

We can depend upon the fact that our loving Father will not play favorites like some earthly fathers do. God's favor may manifest differently for others, but He is always fair and just in His love toward us. It is also important to note that our Abba Father is not controlling or manipulative, and He never takes pleasure in our failure or aims to break us down in order to fix us. When Job lost it all, the Father heard his cries for justice and redeemed all that was lost.

Our loving Father provides and cares for us, and He supplies what we need for our *physical* and *spiritual* development in the same way He did for Jesus. In Luke 2:52, we see the perfect example of the ways Jesus grew in His personal development. It states that Jesus developed in wisdom (mental growth), stature (physical growth), favor with God (spiritual growth), and favor with man (social growth).[1] God provides for all of His children, and He also cares for them. His care looks like encouragement, comfort, and a charge to stay within the boundaries of His grace.

The parable of the prodigal son[2] is another snapshot of an interaction between a loving father and his children. When we are far from home, the love of God calls us from our *pigpen*. Making mistakes doesn't turn us into spiritual orphans, for God is patient and knows we are not fully mature. We also don't have to clean ourselves or hide in shame before returning home. We come as we are and let God's love heal and guide us back into alignment. Adam and Eve tried to solve their problems without their Father by wearing fig leaves over their exposed nakedness. They continued to cover their sin by justifying themselves. They both hid from God's presence and tried to blame their sin on each other and the serpent, a consequence of operating under an orphan spirit instead of a child of God.

Fortunately, we have a loving Father who takes us as we are, clothes us, redeems us, and welcomes us home. We are given a chance to run back to God; however, it's easy to come into God's house and follow the rules instead of cultivating a healthy relationship with the Father. We can go from being a *prodigal son* to an *elder brother*, trying to win

God's favor by working tirelessly as a slave. We are not called to be slaves in our Father's house. We are called to work *with* God, not *for* God. Any religion without a relationship turns us into taskmasters instead of beloved children of a good Father. That *elder brother* mentality also makes it hard to come to the Father with open arms. Rebellion and religion are not the only choices we have. Jesus gave us a third option—*sonship*. He offers us a love that transforms us from orphans to sons and daughters of the King.

The Father *is* fully devoted to us, and we *are becoming* fully devoted to Him. One important thing to notice in this parable is that the prodigal *walked* toward his father, but the father *ran* to his son. This small detail demonstrates who God is for us—our Father. He pursued us before we ever pursued Him. And since we are living in the age of grace, with a habitational relationship, this means that we don't have to go anywhere to find Him. He's here, in our space, ready to engage with us. We don't have to see or feel His presence to know He is there because we have a promise that He will always be with us.[3]

Your communion with your Father is supported through remembering Him. Jesus removed every covering that stood over your mind, every callus upon your heart, all deafness in your ears, all blindness in your eyes, so that you can know, feel, hear, and see your loving Father. There is nothing that can separate you from your loving Father. And your adoption in God's heart began at your supernatural conception at the place of your salvation. You didn't earn your way into God's family because adoption isn't earned. He chose you when you were still an orphan.[4] Jesus gave up His own life and position to take you from illegitimate and nameless to handpicked and embraced.

The new you in Christ is *chosen*, an identity we must embrace fully. You didn't get saved from your wisdom; it was the Father's voice in your heart. He was calling you home. Job felt homeless, and we see him struggle, striving to be right before God. He couldn't find a *defender*, which left him with an impression of fatherlessness. But we have Jesus, our strong defender, who made us right before God so we could have a relationship with our Father! God is pleased with us, not because of our good works but because we *belong* to Him. When He sees us now, He doesn't see our sins or our past; He sees Jesus in us.

God will never stop sending His love signals, beckoning for closeness with us. Moving into a closer connection with Him requires us to terminate any skepticism and replace it with confidence and expectation of His love. Defying doubt encourages us to devote more to Him and abide in His love. There is security, confidence, and trust that comes through the Father's love, where we are safe to tear off the mask of cautious apathy and begin to pour out the genuine expression of our full and trusting hearts. There is a tenderness without awkwardness or the dread of mockery. Let's run toward God's open arms, a place of belonging, joy, and abundant life.

REFLECTION

Are there any ways in which I live or behave as if I have no Father or home?

How is God directing me to deal with these areas of my life?

PRAYER

Father, I know You didn't give me a spirit of fear or shame. You adopted me as Your own, and You are transforming the way I see, think, and feel about Your love. I am made in Your image, and I'm choosing to trust You today. Please remove all my fears and shame and replace them with Your love.

ACTIVATION

Speak the Father's truth over yourself:

"I am no longer ________."

- Unloved

- Unwanted
- Insecure
- Rejected
- Working for approval
- An orphan/slave in my Father's house

"I am _________."

- Loved
- Wanted
- Secure
- Accepted
- One who works from approval
- A beloved son/daughter

DAY 19: YOU ARE A CITIZEN OF HIS KINGDOM

And why would you say, "But it's none of my business"?
The one who knows you completely and judges your every motive
is also the keeper of souls—and not just yours! He sees through
your excuses and holds you responsible for failing to
help those whose lives are threatened.
—Proverbs 24:12, TPT—

INVITATION: IDENTIFY YOURSELF AS A CITIZEN OF AN ETERNAL KINGDOM WITH RIGHTS AND RESPONSIBILITIES

On day 18, we learned about God as our loving Father. Our adoption makes us kings and priests of an eternal Kingdom.[1] Although we are called kings, we are not kings of *our* kingdom. Christ in us is the King of all with no rival. In His Spirit of authority, we live and move and have our being.[2] This may shock you, but the Kingdom of God is not a *democracy*, and we must understand why. If we look at the terms, a democracy operates by the consent or by the will of the people. The Kingdom of God does not work this way. It's not our will but *His* will. The only will that can succeed in a kingdom is the will of a king, making God's Kingdom a *monarchy* with only *one will* to serve King Jesus.

The second thing we must understand about our position as kings in God's Kingdom is the difference between the heavenly Kingdom and worldly kingdoms. Heaven representatives are placed in enemy territory to take spiritual ground, and we don't take ground by fighting with people. Scripture confirms that our real enemy is not humanity but spiritual beings in heavenly places.[3] The King's goal is for everyone to be delivered from darkness and adopted by the Father, joining Heaven's Kingdom realm on earth. God's goal differs from a *worldly* kingdom because we do not use our authority to control others like the political structures do in the natural realm. Our authority's purpose is connected to liberating people instead of enslaving or controlling them. We are also not permitted to use our rights as Kingdom citizens to be first in line but rather to be humble, serving the needs of others.

Our rights and special privileges come from being God's child and are crucial for us to understand and apply. First of all, we must realize that we are united to God through Jesus Christ,[4] who announced Himself as the vine and made us His branches.[5] Jesus then entrusted us with His divine authority.[6] He made us inseparable from our spiritual authority according to 1 John, which says, *"You are of God and you belong to Him and have [already] overcome them [the agents of the antichrist]; because He who is in you is greater than he (Satan) who is in the world [of sinful mankind]"* (1 John 4:4, AMP). Authority is the key to taking ground, and we are each given a portion of God's Kingdom realm to steward. Like Gideon, it starts at home, and then we can move forward. Love (according to God's definition, given to us in 1 Corinthians 13:4–8) is our benchmark, and we need a close relationship with the Holy Spirit to discover how to operate in this kind of love. We also must remember that it's not about us but *Jesus,* in and through us. Knowing these boundaries to our authority is crucial to aligning with God. Walking in authority is the *empowered way* Jesus has called us to live. We must actively submit to God, resist the devil, and glorify Him, just like Jesus did.

In the Kingdom, having rights comes with responsibilities, and they must be in proper balance. The first responsibility of a King's child is to *follow* His Son, Jesus, in all that we do. Jesus declared that we are to be His *witnesses*, spreading His love gospel around the world.[7] The other mandate of the children in the Kingdom of God comes from Micah 6:8: we are to act justly, love mercy, and walk humbly with our God. We carry out justice by behaving honorably, treating others the same way we want to be treated, and showing no partiality. We value mercy by constantly forgiving and pursuing reconciliation, choosing compassion and loyalty to love others. Job demonstrated the Kingdom when he showed mercy and forgave his accusers. Walking humbly with our God is related to being content with our place of identity and authority, placing God as the King of kings.

Finally, *obedience* is how we communicate our love to God as His Kingdom representatives. The first commandment that Jesus instructed was to love the Lord with all our heart, soul, and strength. This love requires obedience to follow our King, no matter the opposition or accusations. In all relationships, there must be sacrifice on both sides. Sacrifice is part of our obedience. This sacrifice has nothing to do with our sins because Jesus covered them for eternity. However, our love for God ought to compel us to offer our lives to Him, becoming fully devoted to serving Him alone. May we lay down every excuse of rebellion and take our place as Kingdom representatives on earth with God's love and mercy leading the way.

REFLECTION

What is holding me back from becoming fully aware of who I am as God's child?

Am I more aware of my *rights* or *responsibilities* as a child of the King?

How can I be more evenly balanced between those two areas?

PRAYER

God, thank You for giving me access to a greater Kingdom. I'm giving up my will today to follow the will of King Jesus. Would You show me the people in my sphere of influence who need to see Your love and mercy through me? I refuse any fear that would hold me back from Heaven's mandate.

ACTIVATION

Announce *your* identity as a Kingdom citizen by declaring, "Today, I am choosing to chase after the realm of God's Kingdom and the righteousness of God. I am a child of the King, and I will serve Him fully!"

DAY 20: YOU ARE A CHILD OF LIGHT

Once your life was full of sin's darkness, but now you have the very light of our Lord shining through you because of your union with him. Your mission is to live as children flooded with his revelation-light!
—Ephesians 5:8, TPT—

INVITATION: IDENTIFY YOURSELF AS A CHILD OF LIGHT SO YOU CAN WALK IN THE LIGHT OF CHRIST AS HE IS IN THE LIGHT

To understand the light, we have to go back to the beginning. In the beginning, there was *physical* darkness. God created light in four steps:

1. God's spirit *hovered* over the waters.
2. God *spoke*, "Let there be light!"
3. God *separated* the light from the darkness.
4. God *named* the light "day" and the dark "night."

Thousands of years later, the earth was filled with *spiritual* darkness, and yet God's Spirit hovered over the earth (specifically over the waters of Mary's womb). When God spoke, "Let there be light," Jesus was conceived inside a virgin. Jesus became the light of the world! In His ministry, Jesus came to separate the light from the dark. He did this by driving out demons and healing diseases, and now He names us *children of light.*[1]

Countless passages in the book of Job show us how he was searching for this very light. It wasn't found in any of his companions. In Job 30:26, he said, *"When I expected good, then came evil [to me]; And when I waited for light, then came darkness"* (AMP). The darkness around him brought confusion. Job knew of God, but he was never introduced to Jesus, the light in the dark. Job also said, *"Oh, that I were as in the months of old, as in the days when God watched over me, when His lamp shone upon my head and by His light I walked through darkness; as I was in the prime of my days, when the friendship and counsel of God were over my tent"* (Job 29:2–4, AMP). Unfortunately, people today in the church can go their whole lives knowing God without encountering the light of Jesus, like Job did. God the Father, through the Holy Spirit, is who illuminates the light of Christ to believers and unbelievers. We don't need to stumble in the dark any longer; Christ has come to overcome the darkness, drawing us to His eternal light.

What is this light within *you*? It is a life-giving light, revealing, transforming, healing, directing, and redeeming our hearts. The light within you isn't *your* goodness or ability, for Christ alone has the power to penetrate any darkness hiding inside our innermost being. This light within you is *Christ,* and it has a unique purpose to transform you and the atmosphere around you. The goal of the light of Christ is to shine through you so the world can see Him. It is not a spotlight for our fame or glory. Any light within us is meant to glorify Jesus's mighty and glorious name.

The darkness in our world can bewilder even the strongest warrior, meaning we must focus and stay on mission until Jesus returns. To stay focused, you must plug yourself into the power source of the Holy Spirit. When your Bridegroom returns, you will need His light to guide you to meet Him. Don't hide your light, but shine brightly, even as the world around you grows darker. You are called to stand out and shine the light of Christ amidst all trials and tribulations, glowing with the love of Jesus.

REFLECTION

To what degree is God's light shining in me?

How can I plug into the power source of the Holy Spirit?

What can I surrender to Him?

What areas in my sphere of influence need the light of Christ through me?

PRAYER

Today is the day I am done with stumbling around in the dark. There may be a fear about what You will show me, Lord, but I'm willing to let You expose any darkness hiding inside my heart. Lead me out of darkness and into Your marvelous light!

ACTIVATION

Jesus is the light of the world, and He is calling you to stay on mission as a light-bearer. Declare your identity over any darkness: "The light of the world is within me, and the darkness cannot overcome it!"

DAY 21: HE IS YOUR GOOD SHEPHERD

You prepare a table before me
in the presence of my enemies.
—Psalm 23:5, ESV—

INVITATION: IDENTIFY JESUS AS YOUR GOOD SHEPHERD

The incredible journey of a shepherd and his sheep reveals the relationship between us and our Good Shepherd, Jesus Christ. There are many unknown nuances to that journey toward the *tablelands* and back home. The only way to the summer pastures is by going through the valleys, which is why David included the valley of the shadow of death in Psalm 23.[1]

When Job found himself in a metaphorical valley like that, it must have felt hopeless. He couldn't see a way out of that depression. We can relate to that feeling when we experience troubles in our lives. However, it's important to remember that just as every mountain has a valley, every valley we face is accompanied by a Good Shepherd.

This means that we are never alone in our struggles and can find comfort and rest in the presence of Jesus.

The tablelands that the sheep are brought to during the summer months are called *mesas*, which is the Spanish word for "table." They are called that because the land is a flat plateau with lots of vegetation. Then, during the fall months, the sheep begin their descent and journey home for the winter. However, there is adversity in the tablelands. Although the land is lush with incredible vegetation in the beautiful summer months, many irritations bother the sheep. One of these irritations is nose flies. These nose flies are not just frustrating; they can be deadly. If the shepherd does not apply oil in time, the nose flies can irritate the sheep's noses so severely that they will bash their face on a rock, trying to get relief, which can cause serious injury or death.

Another irritation is the competition between the herd. Like a pecking order in a group of hens or an alpha in a group of dogs, there is a *top sheep*. One fighting to be the top sheep will not allow others to graze in their territory of choice which has lush vegetation. Unfortunately, because of the constant fighting, they do not rest and become sickly and weak, unable to eat or lie down. If the shepherd doesn't manage this behavior in his flock, his sheep will not thrive.

The next issue in the tablelands is predators. Some of the most common predators for sheep are cougars, bears, lions, and wolves. These predators are sneaky, and sheep are only able to detect them when it is too late, which is why the shepherd must go ahead of the sheep and look for signs of predators. If the shepherd finds a predator, he must kill it before they kill any of his sheep. The last problem on these plateaus in the summer is poisonous plants. These plants are known to older sheep, but the younger ones have trouble discerning a poisonous flower from an edible and delicious one. The shepherd will go ahead of the sheep and remove toxic flowers or plants so the young sheep will not be harmed.

Similar to the adversity on these tablelands was the adversity in the promised land. There was much strife, division, and many distractions on their way to Canaan. The Lord managed to stop division by establishing His leadership.[2] The Lord also instructed them to keep their eyes focused on Him so they wouldn't fall into idolatry.[3]

Later on in the story, we hear there are predators in their land. There were giants in Canaan, and the Israelites were afraid. God had promised to deliver them from their enemies, but they refused to trust Him, and their choice kept them in the wilderness. One generation later, the people of God finally made it into their promised land. They were reminded of the rules God had given them about how they were to live there. They were commanded not to follow idols. God knew that idolatry was poison to their souls, and so, in His kindness, showed them how to remove any idolatry in that territory. Unfortunately, again, they did not heed the word of their Good Shepherd, and like the generation before them, they fell into idolatry. Like Israel, there is an adversary at our table. However, we have oil for that.

The oil of God's spirit soothes any of life's irritations, removing the temptation of competition and bringing us into perfect unity. As for the giants in our land, God has given us stones for them. He has given us authority in a supernatural realm to fight with mighty weapons against the kingdom of darkness, pushing Hell out of our territory.[4] As David came with his five stones, God has given us Ebenezer (stone of help) stones, stones of remembering, stones that tell our history with God.[5] We also fight giants with our identity. They have no right to be in our land. As for the poison in our territory, idolatry is still a temptation in every culture. Satan has done a great job of hiding idolatry and making it look harmless. However, many things will take us away from God, and we cannot tolerate those idols in our lives. Anything that replaces trust in God is an idol. And Jesus, our Good Shepherd, has given us a way to *escape* temptation. His righteousness, His power, His love, and His blood give us the ability to refuse poison. However, if we do take sin's poison, there is an antidote. Jesus's blood will wash away the poison of sin, making us clean, well, and whole.

Jesus has prepared the way for you on this journey of life. He has gone before you, overcoming every obstacle, clutching victory over every enemy, and empowering you to thrive in His land of promise. It's easy to believe that Jesus has saved us, but we must believe He has also *sanctified* us. He has broken the power that sin had in our lives, empowering us to live in righteousness, doing the will of our Father. His table is our communion, and we are instructed to want for nothing else. No food outside of Christ will satisfy your soul. He has made our giants our bread. Every encounter with adversity or resistance will strengthen us, not overcome us. Our hope in our Good Shepherd, Jesus, our Messiah, will give us victory.

REFLECTION

What are the biggest enemies at my table?

Where do I need help from my Shepherd? (Oil for irritations? Stones for giants? Or an antidote for the poison of sin?)

PRAYER

Jesus, thank You for being my Good Shepherd and taking me to a place of communion with You. There are enemies at my table, and I need Your help with them. I can't do this on my own, and I'm asking for You to reveal where You want to start in my life. I trust the nourishment You have already provided. I'm choosing to keep walking by faith today on this journey with You.

ACTIVATION

Recall specific situations of God's provision in the past. Thank Him for each one, and then declare your trust in Him for this next situation. There is always new provision for you, and Jesus wants you to receive the nourishment you need for the next step in your journey with Him.

WEEK 4: COVENANT

But as it is, Christ has acquired a [priestly] ministry which is more excellent [than the old Levitical priestly ministry], for He is the Mediator (Arbiter) of a better covenant [uniting God and man], which has been enacted and rests on better promises.
—Hebrews 8:6, AMP—

INVITATION: KNOW THE TERMS OF YOUR RELATIONSHIP WITH GOD

The terms of our relationship with God changed after Christ's crucifixion and resurrection. In the daily devotions for this week, we will concentrate on the new commitment He made to us through the sacrifice of Christ and our commitment as demonstrated by Jesus in Matthew 22:37–39. Together, they make up the terms of our relationship with God, which is crucial for us to remember when we are going through trials, but also a great reminder while reading the book of Job.

Our covenant is better than the covenant Job had with God. In the times of Job, people had a *visitation* relationship with God, which required them to prepare for an encounter due to the issue of sin. This visitation involved offering a blood sacrifice for atonement. However, Jesus became the one-time living sacrifice for our sins, and all we need to do to have a right relationship with God is to believe in Him as our Lord and Savior, confess our sins, and turn toward Jesus, making Him our Lord. Despite this, we sometimes act as if we need permission to spend time with God.

In church, we often ask for God to come, but we must not forget that Jesus has permitted us to commune with Him directly. We can go straight to the throne of God (like Esther went directly to the king and received favor) because of Jesus Christ. We must also recognize that Jesus moved us from an earthly priesthood (Levitical) to a heavenly priesthood (Melchizedek). In the priesthood of Heaven, we have greater access, better promises, higher authorization, liberty, and increased permission. Our relationship with God transforms us to reflect more of Christ.

When we face hardships and feel like God is absent, we must focus on the terms of our relationship with God and fight the battle knowing we have victory. We must rehearse what Christ has done and keep the whole gospel as a sword in the palm of our hand, resisting hopelessness and defeat. We have been given great permission to have complete access to the Father, and suffering allows us to start peeling off the lies about our partnership with Him.

These devotional days will lay out the terms of your covenant with God and shed light on the strength of that covenant. We have a new and better covenant with Jesus, which rests on better promises. We will examine what it means to shed that old wineskin and renew our covenant with Jesus. We will learn what it means to love God with all our hearts, minds, souls, and strength. And finally, we will commit to God and others in His Kingdom on earth.

In the letter below, the Father reminds us of His commitment to us. He is fully committed to being the love of our life for all of eternity, and His love overrides everything in our past and future. God's promises will never be broken. It's time to learn the rhythms of grace and encounter the fullness of His commitment.

Beloved,

What does the word commitment mean to you? Have your life experiences shaped it to be an obligation or burden? Or have your circumstances made you view it as unreliable and deceitful? You must hear My definition of commitment to understand how I relate and connect with you. First of all, you must rehearse the truth about My love. This love that I offer you does not come with expectations. My heart is open toward you without any expectation of receiving love in return in the same way. I will never use manipulation or coercion to gain a fellowship with you. The choice to interact with Me is yours, but know that My love for you will never waver, regardless of how far you may walk away from Me. My arms will always be open for you, and there is no need to wash up before running into them. Jesus has already made you clean by the shedding of His blood, giving you sufficient grace to meet with Me. I revealed the depths of My love by giving up My beloved Son. We made this decision before the foundation of the earth so that We could redeem you and make you like Us. Our heart will always be full toward you. And Our affection is becoming your identity.

As We travel together, you will feel a renewed sense of belonging, worth, and security. As time passes, you will discover how these three areas have been restored. Your feeling of belonging will deepen as you journey with Us. Your worth in the Kingdom of Heaven will be recognized as you allow the Spirit of God to move within you. As you grow in Christ, you will learn how to live securely connected to Us. Insecurity will no longer be an issue, as I am the true shelter for your soul. Seek refuge in the shadow of My embrace, under the wings of My cherubim, until the trouble has passed. When you feel afraid, give all your fears to Me and trust that your friendship with Jesus will lead the way to triumph.

I am leaning into your heart and laying My hands upon you. Will you open up your heart to receive the oil I am pouring upon your life? I sent you the Holy Spirit as a gift for such a time as this. Will you listen to His guidance? Will you treasure Him in your heart, and will you obey His voice? We are fully committed to your development, and We will always approach your heart with compassion. We are delighted to set Our truth deep in your spirit, into the hidden places of your heart, bringing divine wisdom. We are ready to fill you with pure thoughts, holy desires, and a willing spirit. We want to unlock your heart and your lips. Our passion for you will last forever. It's not about your performance but your willingness to sacrifice your heart as a love offering for Us. Our deep love for you is unwavering and will protect you always.

Dear child, this week, I will remind you of the commitment I have made to you and encourage you to deepen your commitment to Me. I am teaching you how to share the love and blessings you receive with others so they can see Christ in you. There will be opportunities to show your devotion to Me, and the Holy Spirit is eager for you to practice love. Nothing is more meaningful than showing love through My Son, Jesus. When you receive His love, let it flow to others. Remember, love can dispel fear, and the truth of My love brings freedom. You're surrounded by My love daily, so you have more than enough. Come with Me as I lead you onward until the end, through all time, beyond death, and into eternity!

Love,
Your Abba Father

Additional Reading Option: Job Chapters 22–28

DAY 22: NEW WINE

And who would pour fresh, new wine into an old wineskin? Eventually the wine will ferment and make the wineskin burst, losing everything—the wine is spilled, and the wineskin ruined. Instead, new wine is always poured into a new wineskin so that both are preserved.
—Matthew 9:17, TPT—

INVITATION: EXCHANGE THE OLD FOR NEW

The parable of the old and new wineskins is a highly debated passage of Scripture today, where believers debate the meaning of what the wineskins symbolized. Today, we will look at this Scripture with the whole Bible in mind. Our God is known for exchanging old things for new things. This trade is part of His reputation, and it's what makes Him good. Three ways God reveals this about Himself in the Bible are through the exchange of identity, seasons, and covenant.

There are instances in the Bible where a person is given a new name. One of those people we will look at today is Jacob, who became *Israel.* The meaning of Jacob and Israel tells the story of how God exchanged the old for the new. Jacob means "he clutches the heel" because Jacob was born grasping the heel of his older brother, Esau. Although Jacob was following behind his brother Esau, he lived up to the meaning of his name, "to supplant," by grabbing Esau's heel.[1] The fact that these meanings are contradictory is purposeful.

Jacob was known for being self-made, though he often tried to get ahead using deception. He tricked his father, Isaac, into giving him Esau's blessing and inheritance by wearing Esau's cloak and sticking goat hair on his smooth skin. Then, one day, God showed up and wrestled with Jacob. Even after his hip was dislocated, Jacob would not let God go without blessing him, so God changed his name to Israel, which means "to wrestle with God" or "to let God prevail."[2] Jacob went from a belief system of being self-made to a new belief system of letting God prevail in his life.

Another example of God exchanging the old for the new involves times and seasons. Earthly seasons show us that there is a designated time for spring and a time for autumn. The spring is an appointed time for sowing new seeds. Farmers enter the field, prepare the soil, and plant their crops. The fall is an appointed time for harvest when farmers reap what they have sown. Winter is a time of rest, which must take place for healthy soil and healthy crops to grow in the following years.

There are also spiritual seasons. Israel had a season of wandering in the wilderness, which was intended to turn into a season of conquering. Job was also in a wilderness season, where he couldn't make sense of the changes taking place in his life, and felt rejected by the Lord. It's hard to trust what you can't see, and he couldn't see God's hand in his problems. However, the Lord designed wilderness seasons to be where trust is built, and for Israel, He was taking them through the wilderness into a place where they would *take ground*. God's promotion, or call to take ground, was more than just taking land; it was a symbol of how God was going to take them into an entirely new spiritual season. The generation of Israel that came out of Egypt refused to move from the season of coping to the season of conquering, and because of that, they did not receive the fruit of the vine in the promised land.

All of this is reflected in Jesus's example of the exchange of wineskins in the Gospel of Mark.[3] The old wineskins are like Jacob and the generation of Israelites that were rejected from the promised land. The old covenant was a short-term agreement between God and man, which degraded and stiffened over time, much like an old wineskin. This degradation meant that the old covenant was not capable of holding new wine because it would burst. We are vessels that carry precious treasure, but this precious treasure could not be placed in the old agreement, the old covenant. The old agreement was related to behavior modification, as God's people were unable to modify their behavior on their own. They could not follow God's ways because the law of God was written on stone—immovable material.

God prophesied the exchange that would take place concerning that immobile heart in the book of Ezekiel: *"And I will give you a new heart, and a new spirit I will put within you. And I will remove the heart of stone from your flesh and give you a heart of flesh"* (Ezekiel 36:26, ESV). The Lord Jesus Christ provided the new covenant, and it became the place of exchange. God wrote His laws upon our new heart of flesh, and we went from *modifying our behavior* to *operating with the fruit of God's Spirit*. Jesus provided a new wineskin as the container, holding the new wine of the Holy Spirit. We go from *trying to reach God through our works* to accepting the finished work of Christ, *living connected to God*.

This new wine has qualities that resemble natural wine. The flavor of God's Spirit is love, joy, peace, patience, kindness, goodness, faithfulness, gentleness, and self-control. These characteristics are being nurtured in us, similar to how wine undergoes fermentation. The

Spirit of God reveals His written Word, and allowing it to dwell in us is like fermentation. This process is similar to our sanctification, which Jesus provides. Jesus not only took the punishment we deserved on the cross but also removed sin's *power* over us. This exchange of vessels *empowers us* to hold His Spirit.

A new wineskin *preserves* new wine. And this new wine of God's Spirit is kept in our hearts when we embrace the exchange of old for new. The work has been completed. You are a new creation; the old has passed away, and the new has come. However, we can't escape the rest of the wine-making process in our spiritual development to reflect Christ. There is a time of pressure, clarification, and filtration. The tension occurs because the skins need to be separated from the liquid. There may be areas in our life where we feel the pressure, like we are being squeezed. This pressure isn't to destroy us but to reveal the new wine, discarding the undrinkable parts. We were designed with the pressures of life in mind, which means that as long as we operate within our new covenant, Jesus in us will carry most of that load as we move forward into victory. Besides the pressure, there is a need for clarification because large debris needs to be removed by introducing clay. The solid components will stick to the clay, making removal easy. The Holy Spirit reveals what cannot remain, and when we allow that stripping, we become ready for the next stage of our spiritual development.

The next part of this wine-making process is called sanitary filtering, which is done to remove any remaining yeast that could spoil the wine. We grieve the Spirit of God by refusing to acknowledge the sin He points out to us and remain impure. The Lord only reveals to redeem, so we don't have to be ashamed or worried about what is uncovered. If we refuse the filtration step in our spiritual development, the contamination will pervert the quality of God's Spirit through us. His Spirit cannot be contaminated, but if our container denies the filtration piece of the process, what comes out will be defiled. This happens through disconnection with the Spirit, when we try to use our own filter, or if we act like Jacob did, saying to God, "No, I got this!"

God doesn't want you to try to modify the old wineskin. He wants you to understand that He has given you a new heart, name, and wineskin. He has prepared a new way for you to live as a conqueror, which is only accessed by His Spirit. It's time to stop living like an old wineskin and modify our behavior to become more like Christ. God is welcoming you into the new wineskin, provided by His beloved Son, that gives you access to operating in purity and power through His Spirit. Come to His table, and exchange the old for the new.

REFLECTION

Where am I at in my spiritual development? (Am I operating with an old, immovable wineskin, or am I living with a new wineskin?)

What is getting in the way of my spiritual development? (An old mindset? Trying to do it without God? Skipping the filtration process?)

PRAYER

God, I need You to reveal any areas where I am not operating under the new covenant of Christ. I know His covenant brings love and freedom, and I want our relationship to be built upon those two things. May Your Spirit develop me in this season of pressure.

ACTIVATION

Make an exchange with God:

"I am giving You my ________."

- Fear
- Misery

- Chaos
- Resistance
- Obstacles
- Sin
- Deception
- Stubbornness
- Weakness

"I am receiving Your _________."

- Love
- Joy
- Peace
- Patience
- Kindness
- Goodness
- Faithfulness
- Gentleness
- Self-Control

DAY 23: LOVE FEAST

It is a spiritual meal—a love feast.
—1 Corinthians 11:34, MSG—

INVITATION: ACKNOWLEDGE JESUS'S SACRIFICE THROUGH TAKING COMMUNION

Job was told that he wasn't *right with God*. His friends, Eliphaz, Bildad, and Zophar, took turns explaining what sin Job committed to deserve his punishment. Sin puts us at odds with God, and we need blood to atone for our sins. When this story was written, there is evidence that Job was familiar with making sacrifices for sins.[1] He was acting as a priest over his home, making atonement for the sins of his children. Later, Job's friends said his losses and sickness were direct results of sin. So why didn't Job make a sacrifice, just in case? The first reason is that Job couldn't come up with any trespass that would have deserved this much pain. He pointed out that wicked people have it good and receive no punishment on earth for their evil deeds. The other reason Job didn't make a sacrifice is because there was no more blood as everything had been taken from him.

The Word (the bread of life) and the blood of Christ are what provide our reconnection to the Lord. Both were given to us by the sacrifice Jesus made on our behalf at Calvary. The serpent in the garden came, inviting Adam and Eve to his table of rebellion, but God sent His Son, who invited us to a love feast at His table. Now we can share fellowship with the Triune God—the Father, the Son, and the Spirit. What a beautiful exchange.

In the story of Job, Satan removed the blood by taking out all of Job's animals. He could not connect with the Almighty, and his friends never offered to give him any of theirs. Instead, they continued to hurl accusations, judging without any knowledge of the conversation between God and Satan in the courtroom of Heaven. This kind of judgment would be like seeing a Christian telling someone who has cancer that the sickness is a result of their sin and refusing to offer them the good news of the gospel of Jesus Christ. The provision that comes through the blood and body of Jesus includes the forgiveness of sins, removal of guilt and shame, destruction of the power of sin, peace with God, and the healing of all infirmities and diseases. Instead of animal sacrifice, we are invited to a spiritual meal, a love feast called communion.

The blood of Jesus is represented by the cup we drink when we take communion. We remember what the blood did and is continually doing for us. Jesus became the sacrifice, spilling His blood, taking on our sin and, with it, our punishment. Because of Christ, we don't get what we deserve; this is mercy. Jesus sacrificed himself to end the consequence of our sin—death. Now, we are forgiven, atoned, and redeemed by His blood. We remember this gift of mercy through coming continually to the Lord's table, eating and drinking from the feast of His love.

Accompanying mercy, Christ's blood in our spiritual meal offers *grace.* While mercy means *not getting what we deserve,* grace means *getting what we do not deserve*. Grace provides us with the covering we need to have peace with God. When the Father looks at us, He sees the righteousness of Christ, not our failure to hit the mark of His perfect will. For those who struggle with perfectionism, the blood is your freedom from the lie that you can't fail. God's grace isn't dependent on your capability to be perfect. It is sufficient in every impairment or flaw.[2] This clothing of perfection in Christ is a gift not to be taken for granted but to be received over and over with gratitude and thanksgiving. Through drinking the wine, a representation of Christ's blood, we remember how it made grace available to us.

On day 22, we talked about how Jesus's blood sacrifice removed the power that sin had on our lives. Our spirit woke up and became connected to the Lord at our salvation. Now, we have continual intimacy with God, which provides a *habitational* relationship. His presence rests inside us, and when we become aware of His closeness, we reach out to Him when temptation comes our way. Jesus taught us to pray, *"And lead us not into temptation, but deliver us from evil"* (Matthew 6:13, ESV). As with many translations, there are discrepancies in interpretations, and this passage of the Lord's Prayer should be translated not simply as *"Do not bring us to hard testing"* (GNT) but rather as "Do not lead us into unbearable testing."[3] There is always enough grace and mercy to overcome testing. The problem at times is our disconnection from God, which is why prayer and feasting on God's love through communion are so vital to keeping close to God's heart, being empowered by His Spirit, and overcoming the many temptations in life.

The next component of our love feast with God is related to the *bread*. We see bread throughout the Bible, offering a depiction of Christ. He was the manna in the wilderness, the meal flour that removed the poison, the bread of the presence in the temple, and the five loaves that fed the five thousand. The body of Christ is the provision we need for life. Not a life of coping with sickness, but an *abundant* life. The problem that many face is when they witness a true lover of God remain sick or even die from a disease. The truth is that we encounter situations with no explanation, like Job's friends who did not have the full report. We see in part and must remain careful in judging what we see with our physical eyes.

Disappointment doesn't have permission to deny the healing power of Christ, given to all who receive it by faith, for healing is the children's bread.[4] There is a slow and natural healing that comes simply from developing our connection with Jesus. And there are also healing miracles that happen within the body of Christ. What we experience here on earth is known as the *manifestation* of healing. It doesn't always immediately manifest, but that doesn't deny the eternal truth that *"He took up our pain and bore our suffering, yet we considered him punished by God, stricken by him, and afflicted. But he was pierced for our transgressions, he was crushed for our iniquities; the punishment that brought us peace was on him, and by his wounds we are healed"* (Isaiah 53:4–5, NIV). Just as Jesus took on our sins so that our *souls* would be free, He also bore our diseases and infirmities so that our *bodies* would be free. What was broken finds its wholeness in Jesus Christ through His love feast.

Paul reminded the church in Corinth that God's purpose for the spiritual meal of communion was to remember what Jesus had done for them. He said that whenever they took communion, they were proclaiming the Lord's death until He came.[5] Paul had to remind the Corinthian church the purpose of communion because they were taking it in an unworthy manner. He warned them that if they continued taking it that way, they would be guilty of sinning against the body and blood of Christ. The consequence of eating and drinking without discerning the body of Christ brought judgment upon themselves. Paul concluded that this was why many of them were weak and sick, and many had fallen asleep.[6] Denying what Jesus did for us on the cross will deny the power of communion. Paul then provided a solution to not coming under this judgment; he said, *"Everyone ought to examine themselves before they eat of the bread and drink from the cup"* (1 Corinthians 11:28, NIV).

So, before participating in the love feast of communion, examine your motives and remember all that Christ has provided: restoration to your soul and your body. Keep up your remembrance! When you are feeling defeated, it's time to come back to the table of our Lord and receive the provision of the blood and the body of Christ.

REFLECTION

How do I need to change the way I enter into the Lord's love feast of communion, correctly discerning His blood and His body?

PRAYER

Lord, I come to Your table, repenting for any way I have neglected, acknowledging all that Jesus did for me on the cross. Thank You for removing sin's guilt and shame from my heart and giving me peace with God. Thank You for taking on the punishment I deserved, removing my sin, and destroying the power sin had on my life! Thank You for carrying away all of my infirmities and diseases. May I always enter into communion to stay connected to You!

ACTIVATION

Grab elements representing Christ's body and blood (bread/crackers and wine/juice). Once you have them, declare what each one means for you and receive it into your body. Sin came through the mouth of Adam. Likewise, restoration must come through our mouths. God always brings redemption full circle. Take some time to praise Him for what He has done!

DAY 24: WITH ALL OF YOUR HEART AND YOUR SOUL

Keep your heart with all diligence,
for out of it spring the issues of life.
—Proverbs 4:23, NKJV—

INVITATION: KEEP YOUR HEART PURE AND FULL OF AFFECTION FOR GOD ALONE

A relationship won't last if only one person is committing. To have an enduring relationship, both parties must pledge their devotion to one another, demonstrated by hearing couples profess their vows to one another at weddings. God has committed His love for us through the sacrifice of His Son, Jesus Christ, so what are we pledging to Him? In the Gospels, Jesus revealed our commitment to God. We are to love the Lord our God with all our hearts, souls, minds, and strength.[1] Today, we will focus on the first part of that commitment of love—our hearts and souls.

How do we love God with all of our hearts and souls? The book of Proverbs tells us to keep our hearts with all diligence, keeping our hearts pure. What are we keeping it pure from? Jesus responded to Peter's question about what defiles a person by telling him that out of the heart proceeds evil thoughts, murders, adulteries, fornications, thefts, false witness, and blasphemies.[2] Jesus demonstrated that the heart is the source of pollution. When it is contaminated, it will pollute every channel and issue. How can we keep our hearts pure?

The bitter waters of Marah demonstrate our solution.[3] The tainted water represents the defilement of our hearts in this sinful world. God instructed Moses to throw a piece of wood into the waters, which made the water clean and drinkable. This miracle revealed our need for Christ, who was hung on a piece of wood, making the water of our hearts pure. Scripture points out that *"if we walk in the light as He [Christ] is in the light, we have fellowship with one another, and the blood of Jesus Christ His Son cleanses us from all sin"* (1 John 1:7, NKJV).

To have a pure heart, we must protect our connection and devotion to Jesus Christ, who keeps our hearts pure from evil. We must let "deliver us from evil" be our daily prayer. Jesus is the Word of God made flesh, so our connection with Him is found in the washing of the Word, where Jesus told us that we will be made clean.[4] This means that we read the terms of comfort along with the terms of correction, allowing Jesus to reveal areas of our hearts that need transformation.

The second way to keep our hearts pure is to keep our hearts full. In John 7:37, Jesus called out, *"If anyone thirsts, let him come to Me and drink. He who believes in Me, as the Scripture has said, out of his heart will flow rivers of living water"* (NKJV). Everyone is thirsty for something, but only God can bring water to satisfy them. Job was constantly crying out for a redeemer, and he wasn't satisfied with anything else. We need that same determination for a personal encounter with Christ. When Jesus was talking about rivers of living water, He was talking about the Holy Spirit who would dwell in those who received Jesus as their Lord and Savior.[5] If you want to be complete, you must let the Spirit of God fill your reservoir, allowing His love to flow through your heart.

Another way to remain pure is to keep our hearts in peace. We live in a world of noise and visual distractions. But we are up for this challenge because we love God. One of the best ways to keep your heart still is through prayer. Keeping our communication open with God will protect our unity with Him and prepare us for any difficulties we may encounter on the road ahead.

There is also a need for meditation on His Word. In the New Age practice, meditation is centered on *emptying* your mind. People who meditate this way promise that it brings peace. But this can never be so because peace is the presence of Jesus, and He will never require you to clear your mind of all thoughts before He gives you peace. Biblical meditation is centered on *filling* your mind with God's Word. We engage with the wellspring of life, Jesus Christ, when we infuse our minds with what He says.

In Hebrew culture, boys between the ages of 6–10 would begin learning the Torah from a rabbi in their community. On the child's first day of school, their rabbi would give the students a small slate (eventually, they would use it to learn to read and write). The rabbi would pour honey on the child's slate and would have them run their fingers across the slate, telling them to lick the honey off of their fingers while the rabbi would say, "May the words of God be like honey on your tongue."[6] This demonstration would mark their view of the Word of God for the rest of their lives.[7] May we develop this same hunger to both ingest and allow His words to digest deep within our hearts and souls.

The final way to keep our hearts from defilement is to keep our hearts united. A divided heart is a heart that shares its affection. We are called to be faithful to Jesus Christ and have no other gods before Him. James 1:8 tells us that *"a double-minded man [is] unstable in all his ways"* (ESV). Disloyalty comes quietly, like an unannounced thief, to sow seeds of distrust. When we continuously connect with Jesus and allow His words to transform our hearts, we will avoid this corruption. Sometimes, a divided heart can come from having too many outlets. When we become overcommitted to other things, those things, or that performance mentality, will steal the devotion in our hearts that belongs to Christ.

Why do we need to keep the heart pure? The book of Proverbs tells us that from out of the heart spring the issues of life.[8] What we say, think, and do come from the heart, and those things reflect who we are. God says we need a change of heart,[9] and He provides that through the blood of His Son, Jesus. A false gospel proclaims that our hearts don't need to change, but instead, we need to change our environment.

Our relationship with God requires a heart to be developed and transformed by God's presence and Word. While a false gospel demands more education and a new motivation, Jesus has called us to return to Him with all our hearts.[10] Give your whole heart and soul to Christ. He is devoted to you. Will you take the first step in devoting your whole being to Him?

REFLECTION

What is one way I can turn my heart's affection toward God more completely today?

PRAYER

Jesus, I ask that You would create in me a clean heart and renew a right spirit within me. Do not cast me from Your presence or take Your Holy Spirit from me. Restore to me the joy of Your salvation, and uphold me with a willing spirit.[11]

ACTIVATION

The Lord Jesus Christ wants to teach you how to keep your heart with diligence. It's time to ask Him to reveal any areas of your heart that need more attention. Once He shows you, ask Him how He wants you to keep it or care for it better. Write down whatever He shows you and refer back to it often, asking Him to keep revealing what is hiding within your heart.

DAY 25: WITH ALL OF YOUR MIND

I give all my thanks to God, for his mighty power has finally provided a way out through our Lord Jesus, the Anointed One! So if left to myself, the flesh is aligned with the law of sin, but now my renewed mind is fixed on and submitted to God's righteous principles.
—Romans 7:25, TPT—

INVITATION: DEMONSTRATE YOUR LOVE FOR GOD THROUGH RENEWING YOUR MIND

When the Lord knit us together in our mothers' wombs, He designed each of us with a body, soul, and spirit. He set mankind apart from the rest of His creation, making them in His image.[1] We are multilateral beings, created to honor God with every part He created, including our minds. Our mind is powerful and can lead us toward God or away from Him. To keep ourselves close to the Lord, we must learn how to renew our minds. Since the mind is a part of our flesh, it must be transformed by the Spirit of the Lord and through His words.

Let's explore the value of developing a renewed mind. It is essential for the health of the body, soul, and spirit because the three parts are woven together. Words are constantly floating through our minds; some are conscious thoughts, but the majority of our thoughts take place under the radar in our subconscious minds. According to cognitive neuroscientists, our awareness makes up only about 5 percent of our mental activity, so most of our decisions, actions, emotions, and behavior depend on 95 percent of brain activity beyond our conscious awareness.[2] Some of these thoughts are helpful to our survival, but others are destructive and harmful.

This ongoing mental monologue, when left unchecked and unguarded, can develop a self-destructive chatter. When our minds go unprotected, thoughts of rejection, accusations, and identity confusion advance and ultimately drain our minds' energy, leaving the gate wide open for the enemy to do more damage. This ravaged mind is not the will of God for His people. He created our minds to be constantly refreshed with the truth, with living water. A renewed mind challenges us to adopt Heaven's way of thinking rather than how we grew up. Our internal dialogue must align with the language of Heaven, which is God's righteous principles. Below are four simple steps to renewing your mind.

STEPS TO RENEWING YOUR MIND:

1. **Protect your ear and your eye gates.** Faith and fear come by hearing. When going through a season of difficulty, we must guard carefully what and whom we are listening to. There are seasons when it becomes wise for us to restrict our focus by eliminating things that are entirely legal and healthy in a different season. Our eyes and ears are gateways to the mind and can thus affect the soul and body. We can become compromised in particular surroundings, in seasons of difficulty, if we forget to guard those gateways diligently. The following are steps to controlling the atmosphere around us in those challenging seasons:

- *Evaluate activities, commitments, and relationships.* Ask the Holy Spirit, "What is subtracting or adding to my life?"
- *Keep watch over what entertains you.* Ask the Lord, "What is acceptable in my current season? What is the standard You are giving me in this area?"
- *Carefully select your inner circle of friendships.* Remember that iron sharpens iron.[3] Ask Jesus to show you who your iron-sharpening friends are.

2. **Ask the Lord to direct your thoughts.** Too often, we do not bother to ask for the Lord's protection, direction, and oversight of our minds. Start today with a simple prayer: "Jesus, by Your Holy Spirit, keep my mind firmly set where You want it to be focused today." In addition to the invitation of surrender, you must also make it a priority to fill your mind with heavenly realities in the Word of God. It is possible that you feel a lack of hunger for the Word like you used to have and keep, and that's normal to feel that way, but you were not designed to be in lack of anything. Part of why so many lack hunger is the unfamiliarity of how spiritual hunger is developed. In the natural realm, you get hungry by not eating; in the spirit realm, you get hungry by continuously eating and consuming the Word of God. We eat in the spirit realm by reading the Word of God. Jesus said, *"I am the bread of life"* (John 6:35, ESV). When Satan challenged Jesus to prove His identity as a Son of God by turning stones into bread, Jesus responded with, *"Man does not live on bread alone, but man lives by every word that comes from the mouth of the Lord"* (Deuteronomy 8:3, ESV). According to Jesus, we feed our inner man through the words of Christ.

3. **Trace your thoughts back to the source.** Recognize the enemy and fight him with God's powerful Word. If you are having trouble deciding who spoke what, ask the Holy Spirit to guide you. Hold each thought up and ask Him, "Who said this?" He will guide you into all truth, but you must be diligent and ask. Search the Scriptures for the truth, and the source of every lie will be exposed.

4. **Ask God for His higher thought**. Once you have exposed that lie, renounce it. An example would be, "Jesus, I renounce the lie that I can't hear your voice." After you have renounced the lie, replace it with the truth: "The truth is I am one of Jesus's sheep who can always hear His voice."[4] The truth will set you free from a mind that is set on fear, doubt, and pride.

In the book of Job, his thoughts of fear and dread overwhelmed him. He said, *"What I feared has come upon me; what I dreaded has happened to me. I have no peace, no quietness; I have no rest, but only turmoil"* (Job 3:25–26, NIV). Fear is a normal reaction to suffering, but as believers, we have not been given a spirit of fear but a *sound mind*.[5] A sound mind is *renewed* by God's Word. The process of renewal goes as quickly as we allow it to. God desires for us to have His mindset. On day 2 of this devotional, we focused on the Scripture that said we have the mind of Christ,[6] which happens when we surrender and make Jesus *Lord* over our minds. Surrender your mind to Christ, and allow Him to show you how to carefully tend your beautiful garden of the mind. May the Lord shift your thinking to how Heaven thinks. As you persevere with the Lord, may He soak you with His abundant blessing, with His living water that never runs out.

REFLECTION

What area of my mind does God want me to protect in this season, and how is He leading me to defend it? (Refer back to the four "Steps to Renewing Your Mind".)

PRAYER

Holy Spirit, I need to develop a renewed mind. I am inviting You to search my heart and reveal to me any lie that I am currently believing.

When He reveals the lie, ask Him this: "What is the truth?"

ACTIVATION

We have authority over lies when we speak truth over them. Today, declare the truth God reveals to you out loud and rehearse whatever the Holy Spirit reveals during prayer. Make this a daily practice!

DAY 26: WITH ALL OF YOUR STRENGTH

And you shall love the Lord your God
with all your heart, with all your soul,
with all your mind, and with all your strength.
—Mark 12:30, NKJV—

INVITATION: COMMIT TO LOVING GOD WITH ALL OF YOUR STRENGTH

Our love doesn't stop with our hearts, souls, and minds; it requires us to love God with our strength. Have you ever wondered what it means to love God with all your strength? The Greek word in the passage above is *ischys*, which means power, might, and strength.[1] However, Jesus was quoting a Scripture from the Torah that brings a whole other meaning to the word for strength. In Deuteronomy 6:5, the Hebrew word used is *meod*. It means wholly, exceedingly, mightily, and abundantly.[2] From this definition, we can see that our love for God is an abundant love, loving Him with all the strength we have.

In Psalm 84, we see an example of loving God with this abundant love expressed with passionate strength. The psalmist began by describing how their innermost being ached for the Lord's presence: *"My soul longs, yes, faints for the courts of the LORD; my heart and flesh sing for joy to the living God"* (Psalm 84:2, ESV). The courts of the Lord refer to His inner sanctuary, which represents proximity to God or a nearness to Him. Is our heart crying out for intimacy with God? Or do we have a lukewarm affection, disengaged from His heart? Committing to the Lord requires passion, and we must keep that fiery passion burning within our innermost parts. The psalmist continued describing how their heart and flesh cried out for the living God. It isn't just our heart and soul that should desire proximity to God but our flesh. The word flesh in that passage is the Hebrew word *basar,* which refers to the human body.[3] We know that we can bring worship to God by honoring our bodies, which are temples of the Holy Spirit.[4] God has empowered us to love Him with all of our inner and outer beings.

In physical training, there is something called *training to failure.* That means doing reps of movement repeatedly until you physically can't do another. This kind of training is needed to build strength. If we are loving God with all of our strength, it means that we are training our hearts and our flesh to love Him more. There is an increase in passion and longing that comes from engaging our entire being with God. What happens if we fail? Another psalm points to hope despite our failure: *"My flesh and my heart may fail, but God is the strength of my heart and my portion forever"* (Psalm 73:26, ESV). It isn't all up to us in this relationship. God has taken the more significant portion of commitment in this covenant, which means when you struggle to love Him with all your strength, His love will empower you to try again.

Loving the Lord with all your strength refers to the quality and the quantity of your love. Our relationship with God should be the biggest priority of our lives, thus raising the standard of our love to the highest level. Whatever we value requires a cost. The cost doesn't mean we have to earn God's love, for we already have it, and we did nothing to deserve His love. But if you want a closer relationship with the Lord, it will cost you something. We should also aim to increase the quantity of our love. The more time you spend with someone, the closer bond you develop. It is the same way with God. He doesn't require formalities but constant awareness that He's there. He wants to connect with us. Our time of bonding is spent in our worship. While time can ebb and flow throughout our journey with Him, there is a blessing for the one who prioritizes time with God above everything else.

We are invited to be all in, exerting all our effort as we love Him, which is similar to how we keep our connection strong with each other. When we love others in a way that they want to receive love, it powerfully communicates our affection. If our friend's love language is *receiving gifts,* even if it isn't the way we receive love, we can love them with all of our strength by stepping outside of our comfort and finding a small something to give them that we know they would appreciate. It adds richness because the other person can see that we were willing to exert more effort to show that we love them.

God's love language is our obedience, which is part of why He was speaking so highly of Job in the beginning of the story. We please God when we obey what He is speaking to us, for it shows Him that we are listening with a heart ready to respond. When we worship Him in private or public, we can take an opportunity to listen to His prompting and move in a way that responds to His movements. In worship, loving God with all our strength can look like raising our hands as a sign of surrender or moving our body to break loose from the things holding us down.

We can also serve others unto the Lord with all of our hearts. We can serve as if it were just another chore, with an attitude of *getting it out of the way,* or we can go the extra mile. Jesus demonstrated this by washing the feet of His disciples at the Last Supper. When we get to Heaven, there won't be this much resistance to loving God with all of our strength, and so it is a special gift to the Lord to give it all we have got, holding nothing back.

REFLECTION

In what ways do I need to expand my love for God with all of my strength?

Jot down some ways you feel the Lord is encouraging you to expand your love for Him.

PRAYER

God, I long for my love for You to increase. Would You reveal Your love to me today so I can be empowered to demonstrate the same love toward You?

ACTIVATION

Today, it's time to raise the standard of *your* love to the highest level. How has He been asking you to expand your love for Him? Let Him stretch you past previous limits, and don't hold back! If He is asking you to raise your hands during worship, do it! Or if He has been prompting you to do something that feels uncomfortable, obey that prompting! Is He asking you to lay your phone down and spend more time in His Word? Follow His instruction, and your love for God will expand today!

DAY 27: LOVE OTHERS

You shall [unselfishly] love your neighbor as yourself.
—Mark 12:31, AMP—

INVITATION: COMMIT YOURSELF TO LOVE OTHERS THROUGH FORGIVENESS, WORDS OF GRACE, AND ACTS OF SERVICE

We can't obey these words of Jesus (above) unless God is the center of our life. Jesus struck at our self-centered life, calling us to a higher standard of living. Instead of loving yourself supremely, you must love your neighbor as you love yourself. We are powerless to obey that new standard of God unless we love God supremely. The Old Testament reveals to us that the goal of our existence is to have a loving relationship with God so that we might have a meaningful relationship with others. God must be at the vertical axis of your life for the horizontal plane to be in proper balance.

Sometimes, we react to our mess of social relationships by trying to balance out these interpersonal relationships on the horizontal plane.

Unfortunately, the result of focusing on ourselves causes the whole thing to go overboard. We become unbalanced in our love for others when we are unbalanced in our love for God, and there is no amount of human effort, apart from repentance, that can fix that mess. When we understand the grace that God has given us through His Son, Jesus Christ, and live empowered by the Holy Spirit, we can commit ourselves to loving others in the same way Jesus loved us.

One of the terms of our covenant with God requires forgiveness. God has forgiven us, and He expects us to forgive others. Jesus said that if we withhold forgiveness from others, God will withhold forgiveness from us.[1] When we hold onto bitterness, we are not bearing God's image. In the story of Job, he was told to forgive his friends who had hurt him with their words. It wasn't because Job's friends deserved forgiveness; it was because God desires mercy over judgment.[2] We forgive others because God forgave us, which is how we demonstrate love to our neighbors, but it's also how we show that we love God.

We are also called to operate with words of grace. The apostle Paul cautioned us not to allow corrupting talk to come out of our mouths.[3] In the book of Job, his friends spewed accusations out of their mouths with no evidence of grace-filled words upon their lips. Job needed a friend who didn't insist on being right or having all the answers, and grace is the boundary God gives us to bring comfort to those who are suffering.

Our grace-filled words bring hope to the hopeless. When we were in trouble, God's grace met and clothed us with His kindness and compassion. The grace we were given is not to be hoarded but to flow from us into others. The measure of grace we receive is to be multiplied because we are stewards of His grace. We are representatives of His life-giving Spirit. Our words can become invitations to others to trade who they used to be for who God sees them becoming. Gracious words provide possibilities others didn't know were available to them as sons and daughters of God. When we live under that power of grace, aware of what we have received, out of our mouths will flow rivers of living, grace-filled waters where others can taste and see that God is good.

Words are not enough in this kind of love for others. Our words of grace must be fulfilled with acts of service. When the good samaritan saw the man on the side of the road, he did more than speak kindly to him. He saw the agony and the desperation of that man and had compassion for him.[4] When Jesus was grieving the death of John the Baptist, He saw a large crowd, and He had *"compassion on them and healed their sick"* (Matthew 14:14, NIV). Compassion isn't a quality of our flesh but a gift from God provided by His Spirit. It goes beyond the border of pity and unlocks the holy attribute of empathy. When Jesus saw the sick and hurting, He saw things from their point of view and was moved to action by the passion of the Holy Spirit. Empathy leads to compassionate action, demonstrating God's love for others. Jesus gave us the highest calling to serve others. It is what sets us apart from the self-centered world, and it keeps us from the temptation of self-pity. Serving others is a sacred assignment, illustrating the compassionate character of Jesus Christ.

We are discovering how to love God with our hearts, souls, minds, and strength. As we learn and grow in this, the fruit of God's Spirit in us will multiply. Whether you are developing fruit or being pruned, God is proud of your commitment to love the people He created, and He wants to advance your growth in releasing forgiveness, grace, and acts of love.

REFLECTION

In what area does God want to develop my love for others? Forgiveness, words of grace, or acts of service?

PRAYER

Father, reveal anything blocking me from loving others, as Jesus demonstrated. I want to love them with forgiveness, grace, and action. Holy Spirit, empower me with compassion for others.

ACTIVATION

Love is best expressed through our actions. Today, look for ways you can show God's love to others.

DAY 28: GOD'S CULTIVATED GARDEN AND HOME

We are coworkers with God and you are God's cultivated garden, the house he is building.
—1 Corinthians 3:9, TPT—

INVITATION: COMMIT TO BECOMING GOD'S CULTIVATED GARDEN, HIS COWORKERS, WHO ARE BUILDING THE HOUSE OF CHRIST

The house that Jesus Christ is forming is us, His church. The foundation is not made of mortar or clay or a man whose name means *rock*, but by the revelation of Jesus as the Christ (the Anointed One), the Son of the living God.[1] We are called to build upon that foundation alone, for any other foundation will not stand as Christ's beloved bride, His church. We must make our hearts His home, His dwelling place, to become skilled builders of His house.

The home of God is a place of unity where everyone works together under the canopy of love and humility. The apostle Paul encouraged the Corinthian church, reminding them that they are equally important and on the same team.[2] There is a tendency to view the visible parts of ministry as having more value, but the house that Jesus is building has a revelation of God's blueprint, valuing the grace-gifts given to each builder as equally valuable. It is of great importance for us to see each person as a valuable part of Christ's unique design for His church.

In constructing a home, an architect drafts a blueprint, which needs to be followed by the building contractors to the letter. The builder doesn't have the right to change the plan. In the same way, we are the builders of Christ's house, following the blueprint of Christ, held to a standard of obedience. Jesus provides quality materials through His Spirit, but many choose the building material of men, working out of the flesh instead of the Spirit. Discernment will feed you the wisdom needed to tell the difference between the popular materials from the flesh and the obscure but high-quality materials of the Spirit.

We are invited to build using the costly stones of wisdom, redemption, and transformed lives, for those materials prove that we are working with God, not just for God. When we give up the old self-centered life, receiving a new life in Christ, the materials we build with will be transformed into gold, silver, and other precious materials, resembling those used to build Solomon's temple. How we build and what we build upon is of great importance to God.

Each builder is given a unique grace gift, making them a skilled master builder or a top-notch general contractor, like Paul.[3] Some build kitchens, while others help make the roof, and yet others make bedrooms. There is no competition in a job like ours where we build according to God's standards and not our own. We build up the church of Christ under His standard of love, grace, and mercy. As we build, life comes into the home, and unbelievers are drawn to its safety, power, unity, and love.

Besides a building, Paul referred to us as being God's coworkers like that of a cultivated garden, which is an illustration of the Garden of Eden in the book of Genesis. Eden was the place where love between

God and man flourished. If we look back at the temple of God in the Bible, we can see how it symbolized God's redemptive plan—His people coming back to His purpose. We have been privileged to cultivate God's garden with tender humility and quiet patience, demonstrating gentleness and generous love toward others. When we do this, we bring forth such aromatic fruit of God's Spirit that fills the world with an aroma, drawing unbelievers to the beautiful fragrance of Christ. We nurture the garden of the Lord through prayerful plowing, fertilizing with truthful and loving words, and continuously planting the seeds of faith. We also wait on the Lord to water, prune, and weed His garden, which in turn yields abundant growth and a great harvest of souls.

You are a unique part of God's plan, His beautiful garden, and are called to rise as a sent one, ambassador, and authorized representative of Jesus Christ, the Victor. You are God's solution, a cultivator of the sweet, aromatic fruit of love, joy, peace, and all the characteristics of God's nature. And your grace gift and materials are ready to be used by you to build up Christ's home, His church, today. He invites you daily to be a part of His house, become His coworker, work in His garden, and build up His church. What a privilege it is to be a part of the greatest harvest the world has ever seen!

REFLECTION

In what way is God calling me to be His coworker today?

PRAYER

Jesus, thank You for sacrificing Yourself to redeem mankind. How can I work in Your cultivated garden? I am choosing to take You at Your Word. If You said that I have all that I need to do the will of God, then I believe it! I want to be a part of advancing Your Kingdom on the earth.

ACTIVATION

How will *you* be His coworker today? Encouraging your spouse? Praying God's blessing over your child? Listening to the promptings of the Holy Spirit, obeying whatever He tells you to do in the grocery store or the gym? Or maybe asking your coworkers to read the Bible with you during lunch? Anytime and anywhere, we can build up Christ's church!

WEEK 5: SUPPORT

I am the Good Shepherd, and I know [without any doubt those who are] My own and My own know Me [and have a deep, personal relationship with Me]—even as the Father knows Me and I know the Father—and I lay down My [very own] life [sacrificing it] for the benefit of the sheep. I have other sheep [beside these] that are not of this fold. I must bring those also, and they will listen to My voice and pay attention to My call, and they will become one flock with one Shepherd.

—John 10:14–16, AMP—

INVITATION: BEGIN LEANING MORE ON JESUS, YOUR GOOD SHEPHERD, THROUGH THIS PART OF YOUR JOURNEY FOR HIS SUPPORT AND COMFORT

The journey a flock of sheep takes throughout the year is an illustrated expression of our lives with Jesus, our Good Shepherd. The summer months are when the sheep are in the high places, but when autumn hits, the flock must withdraw to lower elevations, toward the home ranch where they spend the winter. Remaining at a higher elevation during the winter months would not benefit the sheep, for if sheep are not kept moving, the pastures will be overeaten, preventing nourishment for the year ahead. The shepherd's job is to keep the sheep always moving throughout the year, and each part of the pilgrimage is carefully thought out and planned ahead of time for the sheep's well-being.

The same is true for us. Our spiritual development requires movement from one season to the next. The flesh within us will always resist the Shepherd's path, and that's why *building a relationship* with the Shepherd is the key to our spiritual well-being. The valley is a place in particular that is harsh for the believer. The valley can evoke fear and cause one to feel trapped on every side. However, the valleys are where we find streams of water, which, for a believer, represent the streams of God's Spirit. This proximity to the *water of life* brings encouragement and gives us direction. The narrowness of this path also yields closeness to the Good Shepherd, who is with us all the way through.

As you can see, these devotional days are focused on Jesus, our Good Shepherd. He is here with you to strengthen, edify, encourage, and guide you on His life path. This week, you will learn the distinction of the Shepherd's path, discover great intimacy with Jesus, exchange anguish for His joy, receive the anointing of His Spirit, and learn how to train your heart for daily encounters of His presence.

In the following letter, Jesus wants to comfort you in your path. He is calling your name, beckoning you to come closer to Him. I pray these words minister to your heart, applying the healing balm of His presence and bringing hope to whatever valley you are walking through in this season. Jesus has all you need, so receive what He has for you today by faith.

Beloved,

At each sunrise, look for Me. Tune your ear to My voice, for I am singing strength back into your life. Don't believe the bad reports of people with no faith in who I am. I am your Good Shepherd, and My voice will always lead you on the pathways of My hope, just as I promised. My words will always carry patience and gentleness. My voice will not rush you or cause feelings of inadequacy or shame. This week is about learning the language of love that I am speaking to your heart.

My heart rejoiced when my eyes saw you in your unformed substance. Every stage of your development satisfies Me, and My pleasure is found in who I am making you into. There is no requirement for worry on this journey, only peace. You have My peace at all times, even in your greatest tribulation. The troubles you are facing come from this world, but My Kingdom is a predominant reality in your life. You are given the keys to this Kingdom when you become like a child, recognizing the simplicity of walking with Me. My yoke is easy because the partnership with Me always brings life. My burden is light because connecting with Me lifts you.

Beloved, I kept your face in mind when I suffered on the cross. You are worth every drop of blood I spilled and every pain I felt in my body and soul. My suffering paved the way for your victory. In Me, you have a solution; in Me, you have hope. Your hope remains invisible until it connects with faith. Faith guards hope so you can see it in the world around you, beholding My glory in your life. Behold, beloved, I have already placed with you the measure of faith you need to break through any obstacle you face. The darkness of this world can never overpower Me, who lives in you. I am the overcoming presence in your life, and you are discovering the power of that reality.

Your worship and prayers will activate that faith that I put inside of you and cause an acceleration of the divine power and anointing that breaks evil yokes, chains, and bondages. May you keep shouting My triumph forever, for I am overshadowing you in My presence through the highs and lows of your life. I am teaching you to cooperate with My Spirit so that you will discover how to trust and believe My Word. You will continue to witness My faithfulness.

I have given you the antidote to all of life's problems. This antidote is accepting the availability of My peace. I am your peace. And My peace permits you to come into the throne room of Heaven, where you will encounter the majesty of My presence. It is from this presence that you will constantly discover My peace. Let My peace go before you. Let My peace become a closed door to every assault on your heart and mind.

My pen has written victory on every page of your book in Heaven. Do you see it? Accept this designated time to lie down and rest in the ark of My presence. The storms may surround us, with turbulent winds swirling all around. However, it is in the height of your greatest danger that I am reviving you, covering you with My glory. Even when ten thousand dark powers prowl around you, we will not be afraid of them, for I am rising to break the power of weapons sent to harm you. I am your feast of favor and bliss. Come and dine on the salvation of your God. I am your delicious feast, strengthening you for our victory.

Love,
Jesus

Additional Reading Option: Job Chapters 29–35

DAY 29: SHADOWS

Those who live in the shelter of the Most High
will find rest in the shadow of the Almighty.
—Psalm 91:1, NLT—

INVITATION: HIDE UNDER THE SHADOW OF HIS WINGS

Valleys are often associated with tribulation, but they can enrich our spiritual lives in a way that isn't possible on the mountain peaks. We, like sheep, need different terrains on our journey. Extended periods in one area can lead to sheep overgrazing, provoking environmental issues. Overgrazing is equivalent to getting comfortable in a particular place where we feel *independent* of Jesus. A good shepherd knows what is best for their sheep and will go to great lengths to prepare the way.

Jesus showed us how to be immersed in Him regardless of the surroundings, enhancing all territories for His glory. Paul and Silas turned a jail cell into a worship hall, and Jesus turned a funeral into a celebration. There may be valleys along our path, but we reach them with the full power and authority of a heavenly Kingdom. The valley King David mentioned in Psalm 23 is described as the valley of the *shadow of death,* which sounds like a place we should avoid. However, there is no other way to those tablelands. Trusting our Good Shepherd in the valley of the shadow of death is the only way through.

A *shadow* is a byproduct of light versus dark, making it a notable theme in Scripture. It is most often used to describe *God's protection.* Physical shade protects us from the sun's heat, and shadows hide us from danger.[1] The prophet Jonah was given an example when he was waiting on the mountainside, hoping to see God's judgment fall on his enemies, the Assyrians.[2] The vine had grown over Jonah, providing him with shade from the heat of the scorching sun. The vine represents the covering Jesus would provide for the sinner who repents. God had sent Jonah to Nineveh to reveal to them that they needed to repent to receive the covering of God to protect them from the Lord's wrath. Jonah's heart was hard, and he could not bear God showing mercy to his enemies. Jonah thought he could get out of sharing the truth with the Assyrians, and his story reminds us that God is the One who provides or takes away the shade of His protection.

Natural vines are a temporary shelter from the day's heat, but we have an eternal shadow of covering. Our souls can find endless rest and safety in God's shadow. There is a definite protection for us when we stay there. In Psalm 121, the psalmist illustrated that if God is watching over us, we are protected from any harm that may come our way both day and night. God serves as a shield against all calamities, guarding us from visible and hidden dangers as the following psalm expresses: *"The Lord is your keeper; The Lord is your shade at your right hand. The sun shall not strike you by day, Nor the moon by night. The Lord shall preserve you from all evil; He shall preserve your soul. The Lord shall preserve your going out and your coming in From this time forth, and even forevermore"* (Psalm 121:5–8, NKJV). We live under the same external conditions as others, but we are protected by divine intervention from dark powers in the supernatural realm. Saints are blessed, not harmed, by the forces that govern the state of the world.

Living under God's wings illustrates the protective shelter of His Almighty presence. In the Gospels, there was a woman who struggled with a severe illness that left her isolated and impoverished for twelve years.[3] Despite those physicians' best efforts, her condition worsened. Yet she held onto a deep conviction that she could find healing in the shadow of Jesus's wings. This woman accepted that if she could simply touch the fringe of His prayer shawl, or *tallit*, her health would be restored. That conviction that led her to the shadow of God may have originated from the Old Testament prophecy that the coming Messiah would have healing in His wings.[4] The prayer shawl that Jesus wore was a garment God had instructed His people to wear to keep His ways in remembrance. The outer edge of that *tallit* is called a *wing*, so by reaching out to Jesus, the woman with the issue of blood demonstrated her unwavering faith in God's protective presence. Her faith in the Good Shepherd put her under the shadow of God's wings.

For those twelve years before Jesus, that woman lived under the shadow of other physicians, finding no protection, strength, or security. God warned us not to be in the shadow of anything other than Him. In the book of Isaiah, God said that those who bolster themselves in the strength of Pharaoh, who represents man's strength without God, live under the shadow of a man-made structure (Egypt). The reward for trusting in anything other than our Good Shepherd is humiliation.[5] What a shame it would be to leave the pastures of our Savior for inferior fields that lead to nothing but shame and destruction. We can unknowingly construct idols when we lean on something else for support, whether they be physicians, friends, or a myriad of other things. Whatever replaces trust in God is a shadow outside of His protection. His goodness propels free will to choose whose shadow we sit under.

Authentic healing can only come from our Good Shepherd, along with salvation and eternal life. Salvation is only found in the shadow of Christ, and anyone who comes without that covering will be turned away at the gates of Heaven.[6] Loving God without knowing and accepting Jesus as our shepherd will not be enough to protect us from His judgment. Salvation is the doorway to eternal life, where death is swallowed up in victory.[7]

The shadow of death described in Psalm 23 uses the Hebrew word *tsal'mawet*, which translates as "shadow-death."[8] This Hebrew word is found the most in the story of Job, likely because Job assumes that he is in the shadow-death valley. This shadow of death is described as a dark and lonely place, arrayed with chaos, without order.[9] It is also a metaphor to describe the lack of good living, the inability to flourish, and the weight of depression. God promised to save those who cry out to Jesus for help in this shadow of death.[10] In Psalm 23, David described the sheep *walking* through the valley of the shadow of death with their Good Shepherd. We actively march with Jesus, the *Light of the world*, into our deepest darkness.

Job was crying out for this light through his whole story; he described over and over his need for the light of the coming Christ. God promised to cast light upon the dark shadows of this world by sending His beloved Son: *"The people who walked in darkness have seen a great light; those who dwelt in the land of the shadow of death, upon them a light has shined"* (Isaiah 9:2, NKJV). You can't have a shadow without a light, and Jesus was the light that eliminated the shadow of death. Jesus is our refuge and protector, and we can hide in the shadow of His wings. With Jesus as the Light of the world, we are no longer prisoners under the shadow of death, but we are free to live in abundant life and peace.[11]

There is no limit to the light of Christ in the valleys of our lives, and we can trust that He will shine brightly in the darkness. What we must do is fix our gaze upon His face. When the psalmist said, *"I lift my eyes up to the hills,"* he was referring to the hill of Jerusalem, the place of God's original sanctuary. But the writer of this psalm didn't say that their help came from a sanctuary made by human hands but *"from the Lord, who made heaven and earth"* (Psalm 121:2, NKJV). Many fears we face can be set aside after we ponder that truth. We are now God's sanctuary, where we can seek His help at any time. He has provided a Shepherd to guide us into the paths of abundant life in Christ. Fix your gaze upon the Light, Jesus, the lamp unto our feet, in the dark shadows of life and death.

REFLECTION

Under what shadows do I sometimes seek refuge beside the shadow of Christ?

How can I move myself under Christ's shadow today?

PRAYER

Jesus, I do not want to live under any other shadow than Yours. Show me how to return under Your protection, security, and abundance. I submit to Your ways and path, even if it's a valley. I want to keep trusting You, so show me what fears I must fling at Your feet to keep my faith strong. I choose to put all of my hope and my trust in You today.

ACTIVATION

We need to speak the truth of Christ's faithfulness in our darkest valleys. Today, declare the closeness of Jesus in your life: "I am walking through this valley under the wings of my Good Shepherd, Jesus Christ!"

DAY 30: LOCKING EYES WITH JESUS

I will instruct you and teach you in the way you
should go; I will counsel you with my eye upon you.
Be not like a horse or a mule, without understanding,
which must be curbed with bit and bridle,
or it will not stay near you.
—Psalm 32:8–9, ESV—

INVITATION: FOCUS ON JESUS

Have you ever realized that making eye contact with someone in person differs from doing it through a screen? No matter how directly a person looks into the camera, we cannot feel the same connection as in person. We can't make eye contact with a photograph either. Making intimate visual contact creates a deep, personal connection that cannot be replicated artificially. With just a glance, eye contact communicates respect, interest, sincerity, appreciation, understanding, warning, empathy, or any of the other thousands of human emotions. When we connect with people through our eyes, we communicate more deeply.

When people connected with the eyes of Jesus, it changed their world forever. One of the ways that His eyes changed lives in the Bible is through overseeing or searching. Jesus looked at Peter with the eyes of one who had been utterly betrayed by one of His dearest friends.[1] The purpose of this kind of gaze isn't to lead us into shame but to cause us to feel deep sorrow over our betrayal, turn away from what led us to deny Christ, and turn back to connect with God.

Another person who was changed by Jesus's gaze was the Samaritan woman at the well. She was a woman looking for love and affection in other places, begging a man to look upon her with adoration.[2] Jesus exposed her most profound insecurity with an offer of giving her eternal security in Him. His eye of affection was on her, searching for what was missing so He could offer her what she longed for. For anyone who has faced rejection and humiliation, feeling unseen and unloved by people, you have a Savior whose eye is fixed upon you. He is looking at you with eyes of devotion and vibrancy. His eyes of life instructed her to Him, her living water. Jesus, full of life, was ready to replenish her soul with something that would never run out.

Jesus then looked at Zacchaeus, who had a reputation for cheating others to make a profit. Zacchaeus needed to see Jesus for himself, and he went to great heights to gaze upon Christ, who would fill the void in his soul. Christ's eyes showed compassion, and he addressed Zacchaeus by name instead of by his previous reputation as a thief. The purpose of the Lord's eyes of compassion is transformation. We can see from the story that Zacchaeus left the business of plundering and immediately followed Christ's call of restoration.[3]

Another purpose of Christ's eye contact with people is connection. Jesus wants to connect with people on the deepest level because of His great love for them. There is a vulnerability that Jesus offers to us, and His eyes are inviting us to shift our gaze upon Him. Another person who reached out to connect with Jesus was the woman with the issue of blood.[4] She only had one focus as she approached Him—to touch His garment. But Jesus offered her more than His garment. Jesus immediately stopped. He had only one focus at that moment—to look upon the one who had reached out to Him. Jesus could have kept going, ignoring that feeling of power surging from His Spirit to someone else, but He didn't. Jesus wanted to see her, and when He found her, He announced her identity as a *daughter* of God. When we receive healing from Jesus, we obtain more than health in our bodies; we secure a confirmation of our identity as sons and daughters of God.

The Lord's eye is always on us, which reveals how valuable we are to Him. Jesus has made us the apple of the Lord's eye,[5] which means God is extremely fond and proud of us because we are His sons and daughters. The eyes of Jesus will not micromanage our lives because He doesn't operate with a goal of control. His goal is connection, which comes from a desire to love. His eyes reveal our identity, but they also reveal His. Christ's eyes are His Word, a mirror for our soul to gaze into. He always reveals to redeem, His gaze exposing our current condition, separating the authentic from the counterfeit. His eyes disclose what is missing to fill that void with the abundance of His love. Turn your eyes upon Jesus, look into His glorious face, and see the truth of His love, allowing it to cast away all of your fears.

REFLECTION

What would it be like for me to look into the eyes of Jesus? What would I see?

PRAYER

Jesus, You know everything about me. You see every step I will take before my journey begins. You have gone into my future to prepare the way, and You are following behind me to spare me from the wounds of my past. Your hand is upon me, and Your eyes are on my life. Your eyes invite me to admit to You all of my sins and refuse to hide them any longer. Your gaze guides me through every tumultuous pathway, and I lock my eyes with You, my Good

Shepherd. You are taking me where I haven't been, but I trust You. I'm coming clean before You, Jesus, celebrating Your kindness. Your wraparound love encircles my life, and You are my loyal companion.

ACTIVATION

Today, find a place where you can be free of distractions. Close your eyes and declare, "I am fixing my eyes upon Jesus, my Good Shepherd." Beginning in a quiet place, where you can easily focus on Jesus, is a great place to start, but if you practice this often, you will be able to fix your spiritual eyes on Jesus, feeling His closeness anywhere!

DAY 31: SACRED SORROW

I can't get a wink of sleep until you come and comfort me. Now I'm too burdened to even pray! My mind wandered, thinking of days gone by—the years long since passed. Then I remembered the worship songs I used to sing in the night seasons, and my heart began to fill again with thoughts of you. So my spirit went out once more in search of you.
—Psalm 77:4–6, TPT—

INVITATION: POUR OUT ALL YOUR GRIEF BEFORE JESUS AND RECEIVE HIS JOY

Seasons of pain and suffering are hard for us to walk through, but we are never alone because a Good Shepherd calls us to discover more of who He is. He is not far off; He is not distant. Jesus is close to the brokenhearted, and His arms of redemption are open for us to run into. In our deepest pain, Jesus invites us to bring our grief to Him. There comes a time when we must wrestle with our faith in Him. When we come to a place of wrestling with

God, like in the story of Job, there is vulnerability and honesty that must be poured out of the depths of our souls.

When we cry out to the Lord, our lamentations ascend to the throne of grace, like the angels climbing the stairway to Heaven at Bethel.[1] Our most profound sorrow was not meant to become a burden for us to carry around and hold on to. That pain must be poured out to make room for new hope and expectation of our Good Shepherd, who will redeem us when we are *cast down*. We need Jesus to restore our soul.

A "cast sheep" is an old term used by English shepherds to describe a sheep that has fallen on its back and cannot stand up on its own. When a sheep falls in this way, it kicks its legs in an attempt to flip over but is unable to get back up on its own. The reason a sheep cannot remain on its back for long is due to the buildup of gasses in its stomach. These gasses, unable to escape, inflate the rumen (sheep's stomach) and restrict blood flow to its legs. When blood flow is cut off, and the heat beats down on the sheep, it can only survive a few hours. It requires a caring shepherd's assistance to help it stand again.

The danger of being cast down is why shepherds take headcounts of their sheep to ensure none of them are missing. If one is gone, the shepherd will immediately suspect it is stuck and run to find it. Like sheep, we can be *cast down*. There are seasons of life that make us feel helpless and hopeless, which can be a normal reaction to our circumstances, but it is not the place God intends us to stay. This was true of Job, for he felt utterly cast down, unable to pull himself back up. The only way back up on our feet is by lamenting before the Lord, calling out to our Shepherd.

The definition of lamenting is "a passionate or demonstrative expression of grief."[2] It is an exercise of faith; it engages honesty and vulnerability with God. Lamenting is recounting His promises and submitting to His will when it is the hardest. To lament is to cry out to God in our most profound doubts and troubles, all while building trust that He will deliver us from our despair. The prayers of lament are both passionate and messy, but the purpose is reconnection. Lamenting prayers lift our souls from a pit of despair into the heights of thanksgiving through rejoicing.

Lamenting is God's design for grieving loss and disappointment. We are not designed to carry on with those burdens holding us down. There is a book in the Bible full of grieved prayers and songs of sorrow called Lamentations, written by the prophet Jeremiah. The place in which Jeremiah penned these songs of grief was at Golgotha, where our Savior was hung upon a cross. Jeremiah watched Jerusalem being destroyed, just as God had warned it would, and the prophet had done all that God asked of him, warning the people of God to repent. To his dismay, the people's hearts were hard, and they refused to return to the Lord, causing the protection of God to leave, leading them to their ruin. Lament is what restores our relationship with God and reconnects us with His goodness. We can stop short of this process by withholding our emotions, hiding it all inside, or moving away from God.

Jeremiah decided that he wasn't going to allow his deep grief to keep him away from the Lord, so he mourned the loss from the depths of his soul, reconnecting with God. He is known as the *weeping* prophet, for he moved entirely through the cycle of lament, which took him closer to God's heart. *Crying* is one of the deepest forms of communication, in which the Lord hears our cries and records them in a book stored in Heaven.[3] Jeremiah released his tears to God, and God released His restoration to Jeremiah. God took him through the grief into a place of abundance.

Counter to this is another prophet named Jonah, who is known as the *whining* prophet. Jonah became stuck in bringing his complaint to God, refusing to move forward in faith. He not only tried to physically distance himself from the Lord, but he emotionally and spiritually separated himself by throwing in the towel and declining the invitation to move his heart closer to God's. Cynicism like Jonah's moves us away from God, while laments like Jeremiah's push us into His presence.

Our souls ascend from the pit of despair to the empowering presence of God through each stage of lament, holding on to God's promises with faith. We find strength in praising God for His goodness when nothing in our current situation looks promising. It is the most excellent offering you can give Him for eternity. It shows God that you trust Him to redeem what was broken and restore what was lost. The path to Jesus is in your spiritual exhaustion; when your heart is overcome with great sadness, call His name so He will restore your soul. Come to Jesus with your weariness. Come with your overwhelmed life. Come with your bewildered mind. Come messy. He's the only shepherd who can restore your life.

REFLECTION

What step do I need to take in this lamenting journey?

Are there tears that need to be shed?

Do I need to ask God for help? Or do I need to praise Him?

PRAYER

Jesus, reveal to me any areas of unreleased grief in my heart that need to be brought before You so that I can be restored. Remind my soul that You only reveal to redeem. Help me to draw closer to You in this pain, allowing my heart to feel all of its feelings, moving closer to You.

ACTIVATION

As you move through grief, close your eyes and ask Jesus to reveal Himself. Where is He in the room? What is He doing? Is He crying with you? Does He have something He wants to give you? Is He reaching toward you? Jesus is close to the *brokenhearted*, and He comes to bring love and healing to internal injuries. When your heart is hurting, picture Jesus with you. Keep interacting with Him, and remember that you have all of His attention; His heart is fixed on bringing you toward wholeness. Allow His hands to wrap around your heart, setting you on your feet again.

DAY 32: APPOINTED JOURNEY

There is a season (a time appointed) for everything
and a time for every delight and event
or purpose under heaven.
—Ecclesiastes 3:1, AMP—

INVITATION: ALIGN YOUR HEART WITH GOD'S CYCLE OF LIFE

When Adam fell into sin, it caused a separation between God and mankind. His sin didn't take God by surprise, for He had already set the sun, moon, and stars in place as reminders of His identity and redemptive plan for His people. Since that separation, different cultures of humanity have kept separating themselves from God by changing how they measure time. Now we have a church that lives unaware of the celestial signs God made in the sky to reveal His redemptive plan that is still in process.

In the natural world, there are four seasons: spring, summer, fall, and winter. Each season, God has a separate objective. The spring is a time for planting, the summer is a time for development, the fall is a time for harvest, and the winter is a time for rest. There is a particular order to each passage of time, and each season is connected to the purpose of God. We can't plant seeds in the winter, because the soil isn't ready. And we can't harvest in the summer before the plants are fully mature, because it isn't the right time. In the seasons of life, God reveals that there are appointed times for certain activities.

The purpose of this separation between seasons is to reveal Jesus and keep us united with Him. In the spring, Jesus became the *Passover* Lamb and the *Firstfruit* of the resurrection. In the fall there is the *Feast of Trumpets*, followed by the *Day of Atonement* and the *Feast of Tabernacles*. Jesus came to break the cycle of sin and death, and He did that by giving His life away, sowing the seed for the harvest of souls. The feasts of God were not holidays for the Jewish people but for *all mankind*. The appointed times of God[1] are God's promises to meet with mankind in a special way. They were a roadmap for Israel that pointed to their Messiah, Jesus Christ. Unfortunately, many of God's chosen people missed the signs and the connection of God's redemption with their celebrations. As they were pointing to the first coming of the Messiah, they continued to point to the second coming of Christ, so there is an urgency to keep aware of these times and seasons as we wait for Him to return. Jesus warned us not to be like the foolish virgins who missed the bridegroom's coming, and He also told us that He is the Good Shepherd whose sheep know His voice.

A shepherd's journey in ancient Israel is a symbolic representation of our pilgrimage with Jesus today. He takes us on a life journey, with moments of connection along the way, that points to the biblical feasts of God. The journey of a shepherd and his flock is simple yet profound. They leave their ranch in the spring, traveling through the valley to the tablelands in the summer. After the summer months have passed, they begin their journey back home. Again, they pass through the valley to reach the ranch where they will spend the winter months feeding and resting until their journey starts again in the spring. The valley in the springtime is connected to the death and resurrection of Jesus Christ and the provision of the Holy Spirit. When a seed is put into the ground, it has to break open for the sprout to make its way through the dirt to the light, growing with the purpose of sustaining life. Jesus was the seed that was sown into the earth, who rose from the grave and gave us all eternal life.

The summer is the time when the shepherd will take their sheep to the highlands. These highlands are the perfect spot for sheep to graze, thanks to the preparation of the shepherd. For Israel, the summer represented a time of growth and testing. Job went through a testing himself and fortunately passed both of those tests. However, Israel failed to pass the test of faith at a place called *Kadesh Barnea* when they refused to enter the promised land.[2] Jesus warned us to stay connected to the vine (Himself) to produce fruit. He has provided all that we need to live a godly life (bearing fruit), and we must continue to protect our connection, allowing Him to prune the dead branches so that we can produce more fruit for His glory.

As the summer ends, the shepherd will begin the journey home through the valley. In the fall, the days get shorter and the nights get longer, representing an increase in darkness. It is also the time of threshing, where the wheat is separated from the chaff which signifies the harvest. Many Jewish rabbis believe that *earth was created* on the Feast of Trumpets (Rosh Hashanah), which takes place in the fall between September and October. This is followed by the Day of Atonement, which rabbis believe is the day that Adam and Eve were *cast out of the Garden of Eden*. Messianic rabbis say that *Jesus was born* around this time of the year, a time when sin had been introduced on the earth. The fall of mankind was met by the birth of a Messiah who came to redeem all that had been lost, making the valley a place of redemption.

The shepherd takes the sheep through the valley, bringing them back home for the winter, where they can graze on the ranch's pasture.

Winter is a time of rest, and it represents our eternal rest, provided by the Good Shepherd. We often miss this divine rhythm of life and create our own tempo that's out of sync with the Lord's. We want things to be done in our own timeframe and often get frustrated with waiting. If God operated this way, we would be a mess, because nothing valuable is made hastily. It takes nine months for a human to grow from a single cell to a baby that can live and breathe outside the mother's womb. Part of trusting God means to submit to His appointed times and seasons. We do this by moving to the rhythm of God's heart daily. No matter your situation, you can find His heartbeat in His Word and sync your heart to His pulse. When you do this regularly, you will recognize the provision and protection in the journey. This revelation gives you hope for your future, and it's part of the development your Good Shepherd is growing within your life. He wants you to trust Him more with each passing day, providing you with what you need through His written and spoken Word to grow strong in Him. It's time to join Jesus in this rhythm of life and align your heart to the cadence of Heaven.

REFLECTION

How can I align my heart with God's timetable? (Is He calling me to meet Him at a particular time each day? Have I spent time asking Him to reveal what part of the journey I am on with Him?)

PRAYER

Jesus, I am in awe of how redemption has been woven into all creation from the beginning to the end of time. Would You align my heart to the plans and purposes You have for me in this season I am currently in? I want to move closer to You and follow Your ways for my life.

ACTIVATION

Are you in a season of planting? Or is it a time of developing and growing what God has promised? Or are you approaching a season of harvesting? Or is this a time to practice resting? Whatever the Lord reveals to you about the season you are in, lean into Him for more insight. Let the Holy Spirit reveal the next step in the season you are in. It's important for you to become aware of the times and seasons so that you will know what to do. This will keep you on His path!

DAY 33: PEACE REIGNS

Do not be anxious or worried about anything, but in everything [every circumstance and situation] by prayer and petition with thanksgiving, continue to make your [specific] requests known to God. And the peace of God [that peace which reassures the heart, that peace] which transcends all understanding, [that peace which] stands guard over your hearts and your minds in Christ Jesus [is yours].
—Philippians 4:6–7, AMP—

INVITATION: PRACTICE LETTING PEACE RULE IN YOUR HEART

"Just pray through it!" How often have you received that response while discussing your mental health or anxiety issues with another believer? Is this response biblical? In Philippians 4:6, Paul encouraged prayer and supplication with thanksgiving, being careful for nothing. Though we may have heard that we should pray through it, this truth is ineffective without the *"peace of God, which passeth all understanding"* (Philippians 4:7, KJV). To attain peace, we need to know the imagery of God's peace, how to connect it to our prayer life, and take our place of authority in Christ.

When you think of peace, the first thing that comes to mind is the absence of conflict. But what is Jesus's definition of peace? *Shalom.* Shalom is the Hebrew word for "peace" in the Old Testament, and its meaning will clarify what Jesus meant when He said, *"Peace I leave with you, my peace I give unto you"* (John 14:27, KJV). Shalom is composed of four Hebrew letters: *Mem, Vav, Lamed,* and *Shin.*[1] The beauty of the Hebrew language is that each letter is a picture. Mem represents water; Vav represents a hook; Lamed represents a staff; and Shin means teeth. Water symbolizes chaos, the same chaos that overtook the world with the great flood, and was calmed by Jesus with the words *"Peace, be still"* (Mark 4:39, KJV). The hook binds things together, like a stake securing a tent to the ground. A staff represents authority, like a shepherd over his flock, and teeth are an instrument to crush or destroy. If we combine those images, the picture of shalom reveals that God's peace means to "destroy the authority that binds to chaos."[2] Isn't that a powerful picture of Jesus, our Prince of Peace? Now that we have seen this image of God's peace, how do we *live it?*

First, we must grab onto this peace. We have three methods of presenting requests to the God of peace: *prayer, supplication,* and *thanksgiving.* Prayer refers to speaking to God in general terms, such as the Lord's prayer. Talking to God this way includes asking for forgiveness and provision for our needs and an awareness of His presence. Supplication is a specific request to God for ourselves or another person. Prayers of supplication are petitioning God to intercede in any situation where the Holy Spirit can intervene. In the story of Job, we see him petitioning God constantly, asking Him to respond. Thanksgiving is an expression of gratitude, a way to meditate on God's faithfulness and magnificent attributes: truthfulness, honesty, justice, purity, loveliness, and virtue. After these three types of requests, a believer can rest in the peace of God, which Paul said, *"shall keep your hearts and minds through Christ Jesus"* (Philippians 4:7, KJV).

The only way to receive God's peace is to *trust Him*. But how do we use this peace to take our place of authority? Who guides us into it?

How well do you *know* the Holy Spirit? Jesus described Him as our Comforter. He is part of the triune Godhead with the Father and the Son. When you hear the Holy Spirit, you hear from the Spirit of the Father and the Son. They are all in perfect harmony with one another. The Spirit of God is our greatest gift, and many have lived without truly knowing Him. However, in our intense trials and through the struggle and pain, we have an excellent opportunity to meet and get to know the Holy Spirit personally.

He comes as a friend, someone who empathizes with our pain. He reminds us that we are seated in heavenly places with Christ above all the noise, pain, and spiritual enemies. The Holy Spirit also reveals how to pray in moments of anxiety and ushers us into a place of peace. When we read the Word of God, we can experience the presence of the Holy Spirit. We can hear the interpretation from the author Himself, the Holy Spirit. He sheds light upon the words and quickens our spirit to trust God's commands so that we can walk in the authority given to us by Him.

Worry and chaos are always connected to lies, so to trust God, we must see that lie, confess it to Him, and then receive His truth as a replacement. If they return, we are responsible for speaking God's truth to it, and *His* truth destroys the authority that binds them to chaos. Take the first step of walking in perfect peace in this journey with Him today, and receive freedom from anxiety and the peace of God. You must begin to stir up that peace that already lives in your heart and release it into the situation you are facing. His grace will always make His peace available to you so that you will always have more than you need.

REFLECTION

What lie have I believed about God's peace? (Do I believe that peace is dependent on the situation, or that I have to find it somewhere, or that it means the absence of conflict?)

What new truth is God speaking to me about His peace, and how can I practice living in that place of peace?

PRAYER

Holy Spirit, thank You for being the peace I need in every circumstance in life. Thank You for closing the door to chaos in my life and opening the door to Your glorious presence where love abounds. Would You show me how to practice peace? Please show me how to stir it up when I'm in trouble. I can't wait to see Your peace annihilate the pressures in my life!

ACTIVATION

Think of something in your life right now that is disrupting your peace. Declare this truth over that situation: "God's peace reigns in my heart, and I will not be moved!"

DAY 34: ANOINTED AND REFRESHED

You have anointed and refreshed
my head with oil, my cup overflows.
—Psalm 23:5, AMP—

INVITATION: RECEIVE THE ANOINTING OIL OF GOD'S SPIRIT FOR YOUR PROTECTION, PURIFICATION, AND REFRESHMENT

The purpose of God's anointing is to fill us with more of His Spirit so that we can be full of life, sufficient to satisfy His holy purpose. There is a need for oil in this dark hour, and God is searching for vessels who are desperate, willing to be filled to overflowing. Jesus alluded to this with the parable of the ten virgins in Matthew 25. Half of the virgins were satisfied with what they already had and resistant to bringing more oil. The reason for this remains unknown, but it seems likely that their hunger for oil had been drained, and their lack was not because there wasn't enough oil but because they turned their attention to other things. Because the Bridegroom turned those virgins away, saying He didn't know them, we can conclude that oil is somehow connected to intimacy with Jesus. Those who had jars of oil had the fuel needed to keep their hearts ablaze for their Bridegroom, and that same fuel is available for the lovers of Christ today. The fuel of His anointing is essential and accessible for our protection, purification, and ongoing refreshment.

The oil of God's Spirit is needed to protect His flock from friction, guarding our unity in Christ. We know in a physical sense that oil is used to lubricate and reduce friction in parts of an automobile. Regarding the life of a sheep, there are times when a flock becomes agitated with one another. When competing for grazing areas, sheep use headbutting to resolve that conflict. Unfortunately, the headbutting stirs up hysteria, making the flock miserable and unable to rest. A shepherd will resolve this by spreading oil on a sheep's forehead to keep this tension from causing injury. The oil on its forehead prevents the blows from persisting, relieving the stress in the flock. Like sheep, we can become easily aggravated with others; we need the oil of God's Spirit, His anointing of love, to keep us from abusing each other and staining His reputation.

Oil also has purification properties. The cleansing effects from oils symbolize the continuous purification of our hearts from the Holy Spirit. One of the greatest threats to the well-being of a flock of sheep is a contagious parasitic disease called *sheep scab*. A shepherd must watch their flock to detect the first sign of this infection. When sheep scab is discovered, the shepherd must immerse all of their sheep in a tub of special oil, ensuring their heads are fully submerged. This oil brings healing to those already infected while protecting against further contamination.

We will never be affected by sheep scab, but there is a supernatural parasitic infection that is spreading throughout Christ's flock, and it leads to destruction. We know this parasitic disease as *rebellion*, and if left to itself, it can wreak havoc over multitudes, spreading its ruin far and wide. Jesus Christ offers a solution to the plague of sin. His oil purifies and cleanses us of unrighteousness, creating a clean heart with the right motives, dreams, and pursuits.

Those who pursue that oil of Christ begin to develop a hunger and thirst for righteousness. When we get a taste of God's presence and power, we won't want anything else. There is no other oil that can satisfy our souls' craving for the Spirit of the living God. His filling leads to our fulfillment. Jesus doesn't just fill us partially; He fills us to overflowing. If you are a guest in someone's house and the host fills your glass, it's done out of politeness and courtesy. However, if they keep filling your glass, you can assume they want you to stay. Jesus is the one who keeps filling your glass until it overflows, sending a powerful message that He never wants you to leave. In His presence comes a supernatural refreshment that overflows and removes the ashes of shame, guilt, and sorrow.[1] Job experienced that overflow in the presence of God at the end of his story in the Bible. The Good Shepherd wants to fill you to overflowing with the power of His presence through the person of His Spirit. There is an invitation for you to be immersed in His oil today, to experience His protection, cleansing, and refreshment. Come to the fountain of grace and receive the oil of Christ's love.

REFLECTION

Where do I need the anointing in my heart? (Do I need protection, cleansing, or refreshment?)

PRAYER

Jesus, pour the oil of Your Spirit over my body, soul, and spirit. Let it saturate my life. Please increase my hunger for Your Spirit!

ACTIVATION

Grab some oil and pour it on yourself (olive oil or vegetable oil will do because you are using it to symbolize the Holy Spirit's anointing, which is unseen). Then declare this passage from Song of Songs out loud: *"May your awakening breath blow upon my life until I am fully yours. Breathe upon me with your Spirit wind. Stir up the sweet spice of your life within me. Spare nothing as you make me your fruitful garden. Hold nothing back until I release your fragrance. Come walk with me as you walked with Adam in your paradise garden. Come taste the fruits of your life in me"* (Song of Songs 4:16, TPT).

DAY 35: STRAIGHT PATHS

In all your ways submit to him,
and he will make your paths straight.
—Proverbs 3:6, NIV—

INVITATION: FOLLOW THE PATH OF YOUR GOOD SHEPHERD

Jesus is the Word, the living expression of God's voice. And it is by His Word that we walk. There is no stumbling in the dark with Christ, for His Word is a lamp to our feet and a light to our path.[1] The word lamp in Hebrew is *ner*, and it defines a lamp as a small clay lantern with a single wick.[2] His Word is a lamp unto our feet, which means that when we submit ourselves to the washing of His Word, it will show us the path our feet should take. The light God shines will not reveal the *whole path*, for if it did, we wouldn't have to trust Him in the journey and could get through on our own. Usually, God reveals where He wants us to step and waits for us to move forward in obedience before revealing the next. We can walk with confidence because God's lamp is lighting the path for our feet.

The light of God's Word reveals *what is right* over *what feels right*. Feelings can be deceptive when they are not submitted to the Spirit of God and His Word. Our feelings should be used as a *gauge* to show us what is going on inside but not as a *guide*. Feelings are a part of our soul, which is in the process of being saved. It is functioning in the corrupt environment of the world and needs to be led by the Holy Spirit to the truth. Our feelings will tell us to hold back truth to show someone we love them, and sometimes our feelings will tell us to stay when God is calling us to go. But the Word of God will remind us that love always communicates the truth, regardless of the outcome.[3]

When we read the Word of God, we learn the sound of His voice, so when we are in a situation where it isn't apparent which pathway is right, we can listen for Him to reveal it through His Spirit and confirm it through His Word. The spoken and the written Word will never contradict each other because they come from the same source. When we fill our minds and hearts with what God has said, our spiritual ears can discern when He is speaking directly to us.

The words of wisdom from the book of Proverbs advises us to *acknowledge* God in *all of our ways*. The word used for acknowledgement is the Hebrew word *yada*, which means "to know."[4] It refers to an intimate, relational kind of knowing. God's Spirit lives inside of us, but are we recognizing His presence there? Are we communicating with Him and listening for His still voice in our spirit? The more we listen to Him, the more we will hear Him speak to us. Sometimes, we get into the habit of praying for God's presence to come down to us. That comes from an old mindset that says we have to petition God to visit us.

With God's grace, we no longer have a *visitation* relationship with God. Instead, grace gives us a *habitational* relationship. It is no longer about being in the right place and time for God to show up. The Holy Spirit, the presence of God, resides in our hearts so we can be in His presence all the time! It is usually a matter of changing our perspective. Instead of asking God to come, thank Him for already being here with us. Acknowledging Him in *all our ways* means that wherever we are and in whatever we are doing, we recognize His presence is there to lead and guide us in all truth. A great way to determine if we are acknowledging Him is when we hear a voice telling us something we don't want to hear, and we do it anyway.

The culture of our world today is obsessed with avoiding discomfort and removing pain. Bildad, Eliphaz, and Zophar (Job's friends) all had philosophies explaining how to escape suffering. However, God's path isn't pain-free, for Jesus promised us that in this life, we will have troubles.[5] Pain has a purpose, and when we avoid pain, we prevent the maturity and strength it can bring. The problem with pain is that it has the potential to further rebellion within us. Still, the possibility of pain removing the covering of self-sufficiency seems to be worth the risk. Many skeptics are born from the belief that God causes pain to motivate righteous behavior. If that were true, Jesus came for nothing, for God could punish us into submission. *Can love and manipulation exist together in the same space?* That question was the problem Job was facing with his friends, who were accusing him of deserving God's punishment. Jesus took our punishment on the cross, and now we are met with grace by the Father. When we face suffering in this life, it isn't because God is punishing us for sin, for Jesus revealed this to His disciples when they asked whose punishment the man born blind was answering for.[6]

Pain is a result of sin, the entity that disconnects us from the source of health and well-being. However, our hope is found in Jesus, who came to reconnect us and heal our pain. Jesus initiated the Kingdom of Heaven, holding a perspective that seems foolish to those disconnected from the source of life. The world's philosophy of avoiding suffering produces vulnerable people, and it generates bondage to a path filled with anxiety at every turn, always looking for relief outside of God. Thankfully, our Good Shepherd, the Bridegroom, is equipping a Bride who is not frightened by trouble or pain but welcomes it, knowing that affliction provides a pathway of miracles and revelation of Christ. God's path for you is good, even though it comes with pain. This journey you are on has one goal, and that is a closeness with Jesus Christ, your Good Shepherd. He reveals that there can be no resurrection without suffering.

REFLECTION

How do I recognize the Holy Spirit's presence in my heart?

Am I communicating with Him and listening to His still voice in my spirit?

Are there any blockages in my heart that would lead me away from God's path (pride, unforgiveness, fear, or doubt)?

PRAYER

Jesus, I want to follow You with all of my heart. Help me to acknowledge You, my way-maker, when I want to go my own way. Show me the path of Your grace, and keep leading me, Lord, upon it.

ACTIVATION

Spend some time in prayer, writing down what the Lord reveals to you about your communication with Him. If there are any blockages to your intimacy, ask God how He wants to remove those barriers. He will reveal any action steps needed for you to move closer. It could be as simple as inviting Him into a certain area of your heart. Or it could be speaking truth to a lie you have been believing. Let Him reveal the next step.

WEEK 6: ENCOUNTERS

My fellow believers, when it seems as though you are facing nothing but difficulties, see it as an invaluable opportunity to experience the greatest joy that you can!
—James 1:2, TPT—

INVITATION: PREPARE YOUR HEART FOR A LIFESTYLE OF ENCOUNTERS WITH GOD, LETTING HIM MARK YOU FOR LIFE

Earmarking is one of the many husbandry procedures of a sheep. It helps the shepherd identify which sheep belong to them. In some parts of the world, sheep graze on open, unfenced ground where the flocks from different farms could get mixed up. Shepherds in those areas put a pattern called a *smit mark* on their sheep so they can identify which ones belong to them. When we belong to Jesus, a similar procedure takes place. We become marked as His sheep, and He becomes our Shepherd. Jesus needs our *yes* to proceed with His marking on our lives. When we go through a tough season of life, where our triumph seems impossible, we can let Jesus mark us. When we are His, He can offer protection and strength along our journey. I became a *Christian* at seven, but Jesus did not become my one and only Shepherd until I was in my thirties. What happened in between was encounters with Him.

There will always be conflicts that accompany our destiny. The obstacles are never there for our destruction but for our strengthening. It is only through those obstacles that God's will becomes reaffirmed and established, but instead of an earmark, He writes His will upon our hearts. We are on a slow, relational journey with God, becoming His sheep and allowing Him to become our Shepherd. Adversities are an invitation into a deeper intimacy with Him. God will never do everything for us, nor will He require us to work independently of Him. Day by day, we discover the gift of co-laboring with God to bring about His purposes in the world around us. We were designed to impact and transform others, and we discover that through our wilderness season.

This week's devotional days are about learning how to invite the Holy Spirit into your daily life. He is here to develop you, bringing light into your darkness and making your roots of faith go deep into the soil of your heart. He also desires to liberate you from unforgiveness, establish a personal relationship with you, and reveal how to operate within His kingdom. We will learn how to become ministers of hope and how to forgive those who have betrayed us, all while training our hearts for endurance.

In the following letter, the Spirit of God wants to draw you closer in your relationship with the Father and the Son. He longs to connect with your heart and asks you to remove your defenses. His purpose for you is growth and connection with God. His voice will never cause you to panic or feel underdeveloped, but it will stir up courage and hunger in your heart to move with Him in this wilderness journey. My prayer is that you continue to develop this close friendship with the Holy Spirit years after you read this devotional. I am convinced that He will satisfy every need, and you will see the abundant riches of His glory.

Beloved,

I welcome you to live in the secret place with Me. Your physical body is in the world, but because I put My Spirit in you, you have access to a place where the enemy cannot go. There is a clarity here that cannot be attained by human intellect, and the key to unlocking this place is your relationship with Jesus Christ. You need to understand that you are a spiritual being, a beloved child of God, who was given a new heart so that you can encounter the presence of God anywhere you are in the world. As you begin to recognize your identity as a child in the Kingdom, you will represent Us on the earth. When I come to you, beloved, I come as a Spirit of full acceptance. You are always fully loved and established by the grace of Jesus Christ. When you hear from Me, you hear from the Father and the Son. We are in complete harmony with the same motives, dreams, desires, plans, and authority. We may interact with you differently, but We are one.

When you are weary from life's problems, I come to you as a friend, constantly reminding you where you are seated in heavenly places. You are always with Christ above all the noise, pain, and spiritual enemies. I want to reveal how both of us can pray together when you feel fear and condemnation, ushering you into a place of peace and assurance. You can experience My presence whenever you read My Word; all you have to do is ask for it, and it will be given to you. There is insight that I long to reveal to your heart when you humble yourself before My Word. Listen, beloved, for the interpretation from Me, the Author. I will shed light upon the words you read and quicken your spirit to trust God's commands so you can walk in the authority We gave you.

Beloved, you are about to encounter a promotion in your life. As you abide in Me, you will go from feeling like a victim of your circumstances to becoming a courageous minister of hope. I will instruct you to keep trusting God to respond with true justice while you respond to Him instead of reacting to the enemy. You are invited to go from knowing Christ objectively to knowing Him personally, deeper than you ever have known Him before. My love for you will show you how to forgive your betrayers and those who have harmed you. As you learn to cooperate with Me, you will shine brighter with the light of Christ, causing others to be drawn to Him and experience that same freedom you have found through His name. You are on your way to developing a strong and solid foundation of trust in God that will brace you for continuous impact, transforming you into the person I created you to be.

When the wells of your soul run dry, and the wind starts to blow, I will help you keep this flame of love for Christ alive. When the light is fading and the night goes on, I await you to run to Me. Run with all of your might into the secret place of our love. Wherever you are, I am there with you, holding up your hands and awakening your heart. My power will cause the chains on your life to hit the floor and restore what has been stolen. Receive My strength and wisdom daily, and be submerged with supernatural empowerment to prevail through pain. You will overcome all that comes against you because of Me.

Love,
Holy Spirit

Additional Reading Option: Job Chapters 36–42

DAY 36: PROMOTION

He never takes his eyes off the righteous;
he honors them lavishly, promotes them endlessly.
—Job 36:7, MSG—

INVITATION: ENGAGE WITH GOD'S PLAN OF PROMOTION FROM HARDSHIP TO BECOME A MINISTER OF HOPE

There are seasons of life where we feel entirely forgotten. Like Job, we can feel like God's presence and His promises are a million miles away. We feel disconnected and begin to disengage from others who are experiencing what we long for—a breakthrough. It is in those challenging seasons that God is transforming everything that's going wrong in our lives into experiences of triumph and hope. When everything feels pointless, Scripture tells us that everything in life has a purpose.[1] There is a promise of promotion on the other side of our wilderness with the provision we need to fulfill it in what appears to be a barren wasteland. We have a choice during this time to be stuck in that season, never moving forward with God, or to allow this time to mature and develop us for the next stage He has for us.

The children of Israel saw God's works but refused to learn His ways. God's faithfulness had a record, and they forgot to recall their history with Him being faithful to fulfill His promises. Out of that neglect, their trust in God was never developed. The one year God had planned for them in the wilderness became a lifetime because Israel went from being slaves in Egypt to being slaves of their circumstances. They became stuck in that stage of their development, and because God loved them, He gave them what they wanted. They stubbornly went their own way, refusing to be led by a Good Shepherd. Our journey with God always begins with a promise, but it also comes with a plan and all the provisions needed for its fulfillment. In the book of Isaiah, we are promised that God is not a liar but keeps His every word: *"It will not return to Me void (useless, without result), Without accomplishing what I desire, And without succeeding in the matter for which I sent it"* (Isaiah 55:11, AMP).

How do we escape experiencing the same fate as being stuck in Israel? The answer to this question comes from Romans 5, where Paul described the process of our development in the wilderness. He said that *"knowing that hardship (distress, pressure, trouble) produces patient endurance; and endurance, proven character (spiritual maturity); and proven character, hope and confident assurance [of eternal salvation]"* (Romans 5:3–4, AMP).

Let's look at Joseph, who is an example of someone who cooperated with God while he was waiting for the fulfillment of God's promise. It began with a dream of Joseph being promoted over his brothers, which got him thrown into a pit. Then, he went from a pit into slavery for eleven years. During those years as a slave, Joseph obeyed God's instructions, and his obedience got him thrown into prison. It would have been easy for Joseph to quit or be satisfied with imprisonment, but he didn't forget that promise God had given him in a dream over a decade beforehand. God's purpose for Joseph was not just persistence or endurance, but those traits helped Joseph wait for God's perfect time. We can get stuck in a season of patient endurance and never move to the next stage, which is connected to developing proficiency.

Our endurance has the potential to produce *proven character*. The Greek word used in that passage of Romans is *dokime*, which means test, experience, proof, or trial.[2] This stage is like a diamond being cut through pressure, and we are told that we can expect to be pressed in every way but not crushed.[3] Going from endurance to proven character or demonstrated character reveals what has developed in us so far. God's faithfulness will endure through our trials, but our faithfulness to Him is what needs to be demonstrated before we can enter the next stage of our development. Abraham showed this by trusting God through the test at Mount Moriah.[4] Joseph demonstrated his character by remaining faithful to God, even after watching Him fulfill other people's dreams. David proved his integrity by sparing King Saul's life when he could have killed him and promoted himself to his anointed position. Jesus was also tested and given a chance of self-promotion, but He chose to do things the Father's way instead, even if it meant waiting and even when it meant going to the cross.

When we have proven our character, it produces hope for others. Now, this favor of God (our promotion) is not for our personal use, or then we would be tempted to manipulate God selfishly. To guard against misuse, we must verify that everyone under our realm of influence benefits somehow from the favor God has given to us. As we walk in obedience and surrender our lives, letting God develop us, we can trust that our pain will be used for not only our good but also for the good of those within our realm of influence. Ann Voskamp described favor's purpose in our suffering: "We can be brokers of healing exactly where we have known the most brokenness. Those who've known an unspoken broken can speak the most real healing."[5]

Allow God to establish you in your pain. This mantle of breakthrough will fall upon your shoulders. The Lord develops a testimony in you so that you can someday stand before someone walking down the same road and say, "Look at what God did for me! He can do the same for you." That is part of our destiny here on earth, to distribute what God has given us. We are distributors of all that Jesus died and paid for on the cross. Remember, the disciples were the ones who distributed a miracle in the feeding of the five thousand. God is the producer of healing and breakthrough, and then He gives us the authority to distribute what He produced through our testimony. We are ministers now in the hardship, endurance, and experience. At the same time, we are also developing into mature ministers of hope in Christ. Our confidence in Him grows each day until we see the fulfillment of every promise.

REFLECTION

What stage of development am I currently in right now?

Hardship → Endurance → Character → Hope

How can I allow Jesus to establish me amid this pain so that I become more mature? (What promise of God am I holding onto today?)

PRAYER

Jesus, thank You for never taking Your eyes off me, even when I feel behind in my development. Help me to trust You in this stage I am in, not looking around but keeping my eyes on You. Stir up a passion in my heart to remind myself of our history together and how You have been faithful to me. Remind me of the promise You have given me for my life, and help me to hold on to that promise with all my heart, trusting You all the way.

ACTIVATION

Practice giving thanks to God through this passage in Isaiah: *"I am confident, unafraid, and I will trust in you! Yes! The Lord Yahweh is my might and my melody; he has become my salvation! With triumphant joy I will drink deeply from the wells of salvation"* (Isaiah 12:2–3, TPT).

DAY 37: TRUSTING GOD'S JUSTICE

At all times they ought to pray
and not give up and lose heart.
—Luke 18:1, AMP—

INVITATION: KEEP TRUSTING GOD TO RESPOND WITH JUSTICE, PRAYING FROM A HEAVENLY PLACE INSTEAD OF BEING REACTIVE TO LIFE'S TROUBLES

Does God love justice? A common question we ask when harsh circumstances arise and linger, seeming unchangeable despite our prayers and appeals. God's role as a judge is disputed between Job and his friends, and it turns out they all knew very little about His ways of justice until God began to speak. The way God operates is a highly debatable topic, a curiosity we shouldn't ignore. Mainly because God calls us, His disciples, to *execute justice.*[1] The words used for justice in the Bible are linked to the word for righteousness. God's righteousness is our standard, and justice is founded in His nature. Job was *seeking* justice for his troubles, and there is an instilled interest in all people to see things made right. The problem is, who sets the standard?

The world's definition of what is right changes depending on the circumstances, but God's goalposts of righteous living don't change. Jesus came at a time when there was much confusion about God's role as judge over His people. He reminded Israel that God loves justice, and part of His justice includes mercy. We all want others to show us mercy, but we have a hard time extending that mercy to people who have harmed us. This difficulty doesn't give us a free pass, and many do not understand God's justice because His people are not revealing it to them.

In the story of Job, everyone is trying to find someone to blame so they can decide the punishment for the criminal at large. Trying to find blame causes bewilderment for a believer and isn't the will of God for those who find themselves in a season of suffering. Searching for justice outside of God for our circumstances comes from a reactionary mindset. If we choose to live in reaction to our problems, the author of those issues (Satan) is given influence over our thought lives, our hearts, and eventually our behavior.

There is a part of our spine called the *vagus nerve* responsible for the autonomic nervous systems of the brain, which controls the involuntary functions of our body. It affects your central nervous system (brain and spinal cord), peripheral nervous system (nerves), and cardiovascular system (heart and blood vessels).[2] Stress is the biggest trigger causing a simulation of this nerve in the body. When it is triggered, this nerve causes a neurocardiogenic response. The body switches from *rest and digest* (parasympathetic) mode to *fight or flight* (sympathetic) mode, which means that it causes sudden changes in blood pressure, heart rate, digestion, vision, hearing, and balance. When we react to life's problems or our pain, it's like we are spiritually flipping a switch that affects our ability to rest in our trust in God and digest His Word of truth.

Jesus is our example of how to live in righteousness, in alignment with God's justice. Trials did not influence Him because He lived under the influence of His Father. This lifestyle was developed through constant prayer, which was proactive instead of reactive. Jesus came to the Father, seeking to please Him. Jesus has called us to live above the noise, in heavenly places, where we have a seat at His table.[3] One of the ways we can find out if we are sitting above the situations we face is by asking ourselves a few questions:

1. What is motivating my prayers? (The actions of the devil or the goodness of God?)
2. What am I more aware of right now? (What Satan is doing, or what God is doing?)
3. Who has my attention? (My problems, or my God?)

Our attention develops a pattern of attention and focus, which becomes the motivation by which we relate to God. There is a lifestyle in the Spirit that has been set aside for you, but you have to rise to where Jesus is enthroned. The fuel we need to endure hardships is prayer, and nothing can strengthen our inner man of the spirit like connecting with Jesus. We need the connection to keep our focus on Him and not our problems. Jesus is inviting you to live more aware of Him as someone who brings justice and stands up for our cause. Jesus is our mediator, and His intent is always to plead for mercy. His heart breaks with yours, and He is fighting with you for your vindication. Christ has already justified you, making you right with God, and He is now working to make all things right for your good. Our endurance in faith requires us to live with a greater awareness of who Jesus is, what He is like, and what He has done.

When we develop that endurance by keeping our eyes on Him, we pray differently. Jesus is teaching us how to pray from Heaven to earth. He is reprogramming our hearts to a new identity as Kingdom citizens and children of God. We are learning not to fall back into the reactive tendencies of our old man but toward the new proactive, relational activities of our new man in Christ! Our minds and hearts are being transformed as we learn this new rhythm of rest. We can live in a state of rest and peace because of our position in Christ and our prayers of trusting that God will do justice. All who love Jesus will see the repayment for what the enemy stole, and we will live forever in the goodness of our God, who loves justice.

REFLECTION

How can I get my awareness back on God and not my problems?

How does the Lord want me to respond to His goodness today?

PRAYER

Jesus, help me to love justice the way You do! I pray for my attention to be upward, looking at Your eyes instead of this storm around me. Change my heart to respond to Your goodness instead of my problems. Show me what You are doing in my life and what part of Your nature I can respond to today.

ACTIVATION

Close your eyes and ask the Holy Spirit to show you what you are focused on.

Ask Him to reveal where Jesus is in the situation you are watching in your mind.

Once you see Jesus, ask Him to come close to you.

Ask Jesus if there is anything He wants to give you in this circumstance. Whatever He reveals, ask Him to bring understanding about what that means, and continue to keep your eyes on Him. When you feel your old man's reactive proneness coming on, find a quiet place to do this activation again. The more time you spend doing this, the more awareness you have of Jesus and what He is up to.

DAY 38: WHEN GOD ANSWERS FROM A WHIRLWIND

Then the LORD spoke to Job out of the storm.
—Job 38:1, NIV—

INVITATION: SHIFT FROM REACTING TO THE ENEMY TO RESPONDING TO GOD IN THE WHIRLWIND OF ADVERSITY

Throughout history, God has used various natural phenomena to speak to people. He revealed Himself through a burning bush with Moses. He carried Elijah in a whirlwind, and He spoke to Job out of a whirlwind! Job's story involves two separate wind storms; the first brought destruction and desolation to Job's livelihood, children, and health. The second storm brought restoration. Jesus described the difference between these two storms when He said, *"The thief comes only in order to steal and kill and destroy. I came that they may have and enjoy life, and have it in abundance [to the full, till it overflows]"* (John 10:10, AMP). The thief leaves a path of destruction and death. The voice of God, however, leaves a different kind of path. It is a path full of goodness, a trail marked by mercy.

For a believer, wherever there has been a wind of destruction, there will be a wind of restoration. That restoration becomes possible because of the atoning sacrifice of our Lord Jesus Christ. He took all of our sin, punishment, shame, guilt, and God's wrath upon Himself so that we would never have to experience those things and could have fellowship with the Father. The whirlwind of God's grace comes through the cross and is given to one who confesses their need for Christ's atoning blood. This wind of God is His relational presence and His majestic power, which brings dead things back to life.

The purpose of the first whirlwind was to destroy Job's relationship with God. Satan proposed to God that Job would curse Him if God took the walls of protection away. There is a song dedicated to refusing the storms of Satan to have any place of influence in our lives. The Sons of Korah mention waters roaring and mountains shaking, yet there is a river of God that will keep us stable.[1] This psalm expresses bold confidence in God's protection, even when threats are real and death is imminent. When chaos surrounds God's people, they can find stillness and peace in the eye of the storm, for Christ's presence is all they need. We have the river of God's Spirit living within us, and we can access that stability regardless of the severity of our circumstances.

Another song that talks about the presence of God being greater than the storm is Psalm 93. It says, *"The floods have lifted up, O Lord, the floods have lifted up their voice; the floods lift up their waves. The Lord on high is mightier than the noise of many waters, than the mighty waves of the sea"* (Psalm 93:3–4, NKJV). The psalmist described the authority of God's power to raise itself against the floods of trouble in our lives. There is no doubt that Jesus meditated on this verse while He was awoken on the sea of Galilee when His disciples were overwhelmed by what their natural eyes could see. Jesus only calmed the storm to reveal His authority over the winds of Satan. We must remember that authority when the waves are hitting our metaphorical boats in life. Jesus promised that the world's waves will continue to rage against

His disciples.[2] Yet Christ also promised that His presence would be with us always.[3]

We see in part. Our eyes and memory perceive the physical reality, but there is a spiritual one that is unknown to us. God's knowledge is limitless. He was aware of the conversation between Himself and Satan in the courts of Heaven in the book of Job. He was aware of His purpose for Job's life and His plan of redemption. There are things we will never know in this life, and it's part of our relational connection with God to come to a place of childlike trust in mystery. We must learn to live with mystery and trust that God's purpose is always redemptive.

When the whirlwind of chaos comes, run to God. The way we run to Him is found in the book of James, which says, *"Submit to [the authority of] God. Resist the devil [stand firm against him] and he will flee from you"* (James 4:7, AMP). Our first step is not to react to what the devil is doing. Our first response is to submit to the authority of God. This submission comes through operating under something called *the fear of the Lord*. The fear of the Lord means we are terrified of being away from God. It means that we are in awe of Him and His ways. We can do this by trembling with love at His presence and by obeying His Word immediately. Through our submission to God, we are opposing and resisting Satan and his plan to destroy our relationship with God.

The last and most challenging thing we can do in a storm is to wait upon the Lord. Waiting on God is not a passive reaction to chaos but an aggressive strategy of resting on God's faithful love standing firm. When we lay down and rest in God's presence, life's storms may persist, but we find a place of peace. Our reward for resting in God is an infusion of His strength.[4] God's whirlwind of redemption meets every whirlwind of desolation.

REFLECTION

When a whirlwind of adversity hits me, how can I shift from reacting to the devil to responding to God?

PRAYER

Lord, be my strength and courage when Your response requires a greater surrender of things; I am not ready to give up. Thank You, God, for always answering my cries. Please show me how to hear Your voice today as I await Your response. In Jesus's name, amen.

ACTIVATION

Enter God's presence by declaring the power of God's voice from Psalm 29:3–11 (TPT):

> *So powerful is Your voice, so brilliant and bright. How majestic as You thunder over the great waters. Your thunder topples the strongest of trees. Your symphonic sound splinters the mighty forests. Your voice makes the deer to give birth. Above the furious flood, the Enthroned One reigns, the King-God, Jesus, rules with eternity at His side. You are the One who gives strength and might to Your people. You are the Lord giving us Your kiss of peace.*

DAY 39: PERSONAL RELATIONSHIP

I'm convinced: You can do anything and everything. Nothing and no one can upset your plans. You asked, "Who is this muddying the water, ignorantly confusing the issue, second-guessing my purposes?" I admit it. I was the one. I babbled on about things far beyond me, made small talk about wonders way over my head. You told me, "Listen, and let me do the talking. Let me ask the questions. You give the answers." I admit I once lived by rumors of you; now I have it all firsthand—from my own eyes and ears! I'm sorry—forgive me. I'll never do that again, I promise! I'll never again live on crusts of hearsay, crumbs of rumor.

—Job 42:1–6, MSG—

INVITATION: GO FROM KNOWING CHRIST OBJECTIVELY TO KNOWING CHRIST PERSONALLY

The Lord's original intention was for a relationship between Himself and all of humanity. Unfortunately, everyone rejected Him over and over and over. So, He chose Abram and built a nation to show the world His desires and intentions for all. In the book of Genesis, we see God taking Abram on a journey from knowing about Him to knowing Him through experience. We are on the same journey today, illustrated through a photograph and menu.

When we look at a photograph of a person, we obtain information about them on an objective level—the color of their eyes, their height, hair color, general appearance, etc. We see the way their smile produces dimples, or we might understand their preference in clothing from what they are wearing in the picture. But even if we study the photograph in detail, gathering all the information we can from it, we can only achieve outward, objective knowledge of that person. That is it. We can only say we know some things about the person and their appearance. However, we cannot say we really know them. Now, let's say we meet the person from the photograph face-to-face. We see their peculiarities, we hear the way they talk, and we learn how they act around us. As we spend time with them, we begin a journey of knowing them personally. If we continue to spend time around them, we will become acquainted with their thoughts, feelings, dreams, likes, dislikes, and whole personalities. Knowing them that way is entirely different from simply knowing about them through studying their photograph. This kind of knowledge is personal, subjective, and firsthand.

We are after that personal knowledge with our relationship with the Lord. Because His Spirit dwells in us, we can know Christ personally. When we receive Christ, He saves us from God's judgment, but He also comes to live within us. The Spirit of God dwells in our spirit, the deepest part of our being, and regenerates it with His divine life. Christ today is with us in our spirit! We can know Christ personally—His likes and dislikes, His personality, His ways—by fellowshipping with Him in our spirit. No one could be closer or more available to us than the Lord is in our spirit. We can talk with Him, love Him, and enjoy His presence in our spirit. By taking time to be with Him in prayer, we can know the Lord in a personal, authentic, and genuine way. As the Spirit in us, He leads us into the reality of who and what He is to us.

Another illustration to show the difference between knowing about something and knowing something by experience can be summarized by pondering the difference between a description in a menu and eating a dish at a restaurant. A person can go to a restaurant and read about a particular dish from a menu pamphlet. Thinking it sounds delicious, they can ask the server everything about that dish—how it's prepared, how long it takes to cook, the history of the dish, the ingredient list, and so on. But even after all that, the person can only know about that dish objectively and will still be hungry. They could claim to know about that food, but what good is that knowledge if they are still hungry? To satisfy our hunger, we must eat food. The only way to honestly know food is by personal experience. When we eat, we know the taste, the smell, and even better, how it makes us feel. It strengthens us as we digest and absorb the nutrients into our bodies.

The menu and the food relate to God's written Word and His presence. What is the purpose of a menu? Do menus exist for us to memorize and study only? Or do they guide us to foods that satisfy our hunger? The only way to truly satisfy our hunger is to meet with the God we read about in His Word. Jesus told us that He is the bread of life; whoever comes to Him will not be hungry, and whoever believes in Him will not be thirsty.[1] This is because Jesus is the one who satisfies our spiritual hunger and thirst when we come to meet Him personally.

The Word of God is a divine instrument meant to keep us longing for Jesus, not to be cast aside. When we read the Old or the New Testament, the Spirit of God speaks to us more about the beauty and majesty of Christ. The Lord desires us to know Him subjectively in the same way we know bread by eating. When Jesus commanded His followers to eat His flesh, He was not speaking of them physically eating His body. If we look further in the passage, we see Jesus explain it to us: *"It is the Spirit who gives life; the flesh profits nothing. The words that I speak to you are spirit, and they are life"* (John 6:63, NKJV). So, we ingest the light of the Lord Jesus by taking His Word into us as spirit and life, digesting what He said, and absorbing it into our inner man of the spirit, where it will influence our actions. Consuming the Word is how we know Jesus as our spiritual food, one that satisfies and brings life.

How do we go from knowing Him objectively to knowing Him personally? Ephesians 6:17–18 tells us to receive *"the mighty razor-sharp Spirit-sword of the spoken word of God. Pray passionately in the Spirit, as you constantly intercede with every form of prayer at all times"* (TPT). These verses, along with those from John 6, show us that the way to receive the Word as spirit and life is by *prayer*. If we come to the Word only to study it, we will, at best, learn something about the Lord Jesus. But when we exercise our spirit by praying with the words from the Bible, we touch and receive the Spirit who gives life.

We have the Lord as the Spirit indwelling us, and every day is a new opportunity for us to know Him personally. When we spend time to fellowship with Him and contact Him in our spirit each day, we get to know more than a *photograph* of Jesus; we get to know a *real and living person*, personally and subjectively. Moreover, as we daily exercise to pray with God's Word, His words become spirit and life to us. As we eat the Word in this way, Jesus becomes our very life supply, and we come to know Christ deeply and inwardly.

REFLECTION

What do I need to lay down to know Jesus in a more personal, authentic, and genuine way?

PRAYER

Jesus, I need to experience You for myself today. As I take in Your Word, I ask Your Spirit to awaken my spirit and show me how to eat Your Word. I desire to taste and see that You are good today! Reveal Yourself to me, Lord. I need to see You!

ACTIVATION

Eating God's Word means that we consider it often. We take time to chew on it. Ask the Lord to reveal what part of His Word He wants you to meditate on. When He shows you, read it often. Put it somewhere you will see it, and ponder that Word while cleaning the dishes, driving to church, or taking a walk. Let Him show you what that passage means for your life, and let it stir up a hunger to know more about Jesus.

DAY 40: FORGIVENESS BRINGS LIBERTY

The LORD restored the fortunes of Job when he prayed for his friends, and the LORD gave Job twice as much as he had before.
—Job 42:10, AMP—

INVITATION: FORGIVE YOUR BETRAYERS AND RECEIVE GOD'S FREEDOM AND FORGIVENESS

We will, at one time or another, cross paths with something called betrayal, which can become a costly encounter. The battle that ensues within this confrontation can leave some open wounds. Some of these wounds are so deep that every time you move, the intense pain triggers memories, and you relive their betrayal as if it were a fresh wound. When we walk around with these open injuries, there is an unseen trail of blood that follows us everywhere we go. Like a hurt animal, anyone could follow the path to see us licking our wounds on the side of the road.

Along this trail of tears and pain, our first responder is always Jesus. He knows His sheep. Jesus is present whenever we encounter pain and disappointment, and He is there with healing and open arms. Unfortunately, there is someone else who can smell the wounds from a betrayal, an enemy who seeks to steal, kill, and destroy. The enemy comes and offers something that our flesh desires, like that of Adam and Eve in the garden. He offers revenge, bitterness, and disappointment. It feels good at first, but after a while, the harshness of that forbidden fruit overpowers us, and we are left with a rottenness in our mouths.

It is crucial to be aware of the two responders when we are hurt. Both are holding these apples that look delicious, but one of them is spoiled and poisonous on the inside. We must know which one is which. We must know the voice of our Shepherd and follow Him always, even when He compels us to do what makes us uncomfortable, like forgiving someone who harmed us. Getting even will never lead to healing; it will only destroy us. Holding onto hurts will never heal our wounds. So, what will heal us? The Bible says that healing comes by giving the Good Shepherd access to our wounds and letting Him apply His forgiveness so that we can apply forgiveness to others.

The only way to truly forgive someone who has wronged us and is not apologetic is to look inward. That may sound strange, but it is the truth. When we invite the Lord to search our hearts with the presence of Jesus, God exposes our rejection of repentance and betrayal of Him. Of course, this is not in a shaming, condemning way but a transforming way. With that exposure comes this unveiling of an undeserved forgiveness, an extravagant grace. When we recognize the grace that we have received from God, the cross beckons us to extend grace to others. Forgiveness is never deserved, and if you are waiting for an apology to forgive, you may never get the chance to receive freedom from the chains of bondage that come with unforgiveness. Bitterness is a yoke of slavery that we should not wear in our daily walk with Christ. The apostle Paul reminded us of this in Galatians:

"For freedom Christ has set us free; stand firm therefore, and do not submit again to a yoke of slavery" (Galatians 5:1, ESV).

Paul saw the division destroying the church in Galatia, and he addressed it by asking, *"You were running well. Who hindered you from obeying the truth?"* (Galatians 5:7, ESV). Unforgiveness can hinder our walk, and we can go through life unaware of its destruction. Paul told the church, *"This persuasion is not from him who calls you"* (Galatians 5:8, ESV). He pointed out to them that the voice they were listening to was not from their Good Shepherd. The Galatian church needed to fix its eyes on Jesus and allow Him to perfect their faith. And that is how we forgive—by understanding how we have been forgiven and allowing the Lord to complete the work in us. Forgiveness is a choice, and on our own, we will fail to choose to forgive time and time again. It is only through the power of the blood of Jesus that we can forgive those who have betrayed us and inflicted deep wounds on our souls.

REFLECTION

Who do I need to release forgiveness to?

PRAYER

Lord, I want to see Your face today. Draw me closer to You. My spirit seeks to walk the narrow path of righteousness, and I know that I cannot do it in my strength. So today, I am asking for the power that I know can only be found in You to forgive those who have betrayed me. I desire liberty that comes through the cross, and I am so tired and weary of carrying this heavy burden of unforgiveness in my heart. I am here to ask for Your help in healing the wounds caused by the betrayal of friends and family. Today, I release forgiveness to those who have hurt me the most, and I am asking You, Lord, to help me, little by little, give away the bitterness until the sweetness of liberty and freedom returns. Thank You, God, for Your mercy. I desire to become that open vessel that overflows what has been poured into me. As You have mercy on me, let that mercy overflow to others. In Jesus's name, amen.

ACTIVATION

Write down the names of people who you need to forgive. Once you have written those names down, forgive them by name, release them from punishment, and ask God to help you to continue to release them in the future. When you have finished, toss that list of names in the fire. This exercise helps us understand that their sins are forgiven, so we cannot hold those sins against them anymore. It releases us from judgment because God cannot forgive us when we are holding unforgiveness toward others.[1] Today is a day to experience the freedom that comes through forgiveness!

DAY 41: LIGHT IN THE DARKNESS

The people walking in darkness have seen
a great light; on those living in the land
of deep darkness a light has dawned.
—Isaiah 9:2, NIV—

INVITATION: LET CHRIST'S LIGHT SHINE THROUGH YOU WHEREVER YOU ARE

The book of Job was set when there were whispers of God, but there was a lack of encounter. As Job went through the tunnel of suffering, stumbling in the dark, a beacon of light pierced that darkness. The purpose of the book of Job is not to develop a theology that seeks to explain why bad things happen but to implore us to seek out the light in the darkness. That light has come in human form; His name is Jesus.

In the Gospel of John, Jesus described himself as the fulfillment of prophecy through Isaiah when He said, *"I am the light of the world. Whoever follows me will not walk in darkness, but will have the light of life"*

(John 8:12, ESV). Jesus came as the light, but He also came to turn on the light inside of all of us. He dwells in you. As you read His Word and allow God to develop you, the light in you gets brighter and brighter. Mathew 5:14 says, *"You are the light of the world."* When the light gets turned on inside us, darkness has no choice but to flee. Jesus provided two metaphors to describe this light.

The first metaphor is a *city on a hill* from Matthew 5:14: *"You are the light of the world. A city set on a hill cannot be hidden."* We are a city on a hill that should not be hidden from the world. A city on a hill is not a man-made structure but a supernatural community built on the foundation of the knowledge of Christ. We don't become a city on a hill by elevating ourselves to be seen; instead, to get higher, we must come lower. As we demonstrate humility and faithfulness to God, He will set us up on a hill, visible to the world. Jesus living in us should not be the biggest secret in our homes, offices, neighborhoods, or even on our social media pages. This analogy is broad, an aerial perspective of our impact on the world around us.

Impacting the world today goes beyond inviting people to church. It means that we are all called to show love to our communities by walking in the opposite spirit. When the world is divisive, a city on a hill walks in unity, not allowing the issues to rise above the call to love and honor one another. When the world feeds on fear, a city on a hill provides the truth in love, revealing the lies fueling that fear so that people can experience freedom. Each of us individually becomes the lit-up city on a hill when we walk in the opposite spirit.

In addition to a city on a hill, Jesus likened us to a lamp. Matthew 5:15 says, *"Nor do people light a lamp and put it under a basket, but on a stand, and it gives light to all in the house"* (ESV). Unfortunately, many Christians hide their light under a basket by trying to blend in with the crowd. What the light of Christ touches, it aims to transform, and there are many around us resistant to that transformation. Are we willing to shine our light around those who are uncomfortable with what the light exposes? It can be uncomfortable when our light glows brightly in the darkness; yet, as the moon reflects the light of the sun, so are we to reflect the light of Christ. Our light helps others to find Him, no matter how uneasy it makes the crowd.

When we allow His light to shine brightly, it illuminates the pathway to salvation for those around us. As the earth reveals the glory of God, so does the light within you. As you shine, unbelievers will recognize their deep need for Jesus. His light in you can transform your home, workplace, neighborhood, and world to find supernatural hope, love, and eternal life through Jesus Christ. Let's illuminate the world with Him!

REFLECTION

Think about atmospheres around you that are dark. How can you shine brightly there? (Don't make it complicated—just start!)

PRAYER

Jesus, make Yourself at home in me! I am opening the door for You to stay! Come in!

ACTIVATION

Declare this truth today: "I am the light of Christ today in ________." (name where you will shine His light).

DAY 42: DEEPLY ROOTED AND BRACING FOR IMPACT

In the same way you received Jesus our Lord and Messiah by faith, continue your journey of faith, progressing further into your union with him! Your spiritual roots go deeply into his life as you are continually infused with strength, encouraged in every way. For you are established in the faith you have absorbed and enriched by your devotion to him!

—Colossians 2:6–7, TPT—

INVITATION: PERSIST IN DEVELOPING A STRONG, UNSEEN FOUNDATION OF TRUST IN GOD THAT WILL BRACE YOU FOR ENCOUNTERING HIS PRESENCE

There is a stunning link between the growth of a Chinese bamboo tree and the development of our confidence in God. Like our faith, the Chinese bamboo tree requires a lot of nurturing, just like our faith. When it is planted from a seed and given water and fertilizer for a whole year, nothing happens above the ground. There are no signs of growth. Another year goes by, and nothing changes. Then, three or four years go by, and still, nothing. Can you imagine the frustration you would feel seeing no progress? It would be easy to presume the seeds were duds, incapable of maturing into trees. Then, finally, in the fifth year of caring for it, something remarkable occurs. The Chinese bamboo tree grows ninety feet in only six weeks! Unbeknownst to anyone, the bamboo had spent five years developing a root system strong enough to support outward growth in that fifth year and beyond.

Had that tree not developed a solid, unseen foundation, it could not have sustained its future tall structure. We are the same way with our journey of faith. Some seeds are placed in the ground through prayer without outward growth being detected for years. We see Job continuously going to God with requests, expecting God to answer him. Prayer helps us move into a deeper trust in the Lord and stay in that place of confidence, remaining diligent in seeking Him alone. During a waiting period, between the promise and its fulfillment, we can count on God's involvement. God told us that He is watching over His Word to perform it.[1] God is dedicated to the Word He has spoken over you, and He will develop it in your heart until it bears the fruit of His Spirit.

We must fill our minds with what He has said and listen to what He is saying now. Our persistence in prayer is crucial to the breakthroughs God designed for our lives. In this, we must learn how to go to war using the Word. Jesus said, *"As for what was sown on good soil, this is the one who hears the word and understands it. He indeed bears fruit and yields, in one case a hundredfold, in another sixty, and in another thirty"* (Matthew 13:23, ESV). Speaking what God has said over your life is the only thing that puts a sword in your hand in this supernatural battle you are facing. You must release the Word through your mouth with the fuel of faith to wield that mighty weapon. When we decree God's Word with our mouths, His Word becomes established in our lives.[2]

God established the world with decrees. He spoke, and what was spoken was created. Psalm 148:6 declares, *"And he established them forever and ever; he gave a decree, and it shall not pass away"* (Psalm 148:6, ESV). And because we are made in His image, we can do as our Father does. We have the power to decree His Word in faith, trusting that in due time, God will perform it.

REFLECTION

In what ways can I build a foundation of trust as I wait on the Lord?

PRAYER

Thank You, God, for the root system I cannot see. I trust that it is growing as I diligently seek You with all my heart.

ACTIVATION

Are you ready to experience the supernatural impact of God's presence on a regular basis? His love and strength are waiting to overwhelm and empower you. It's important to set aside dedicated time to seek the Lord beyond daily devotionals. Lingering in God's presence doesn't just happen, for you will have to make a commitment to enter that sacred space and linger there. This shouldn't be done in a legalistic manner, as a mere obligation, but in a way that slowly opens you up to craving that time with God, needing it more than you need to accomplish your never-ending tasks. Once you reach that place of craving more time with Him, you will discover that His presence is life-giving! Your roots will go deep when you linger in God's presence often, and it will become the new rhythm of your life. This sacred space with God will transform you, and you will begin to see Him and experience Him everywhere you go.

NOTES

DAY 1: READY TO RESCUE YOU

1. Henderson, Robert. "Session 1: Three Dimensions of Prayer: Father, Friend, and Judge." Christian Learning. Accessed August 28, 2023. https://courses.christianlearning.com/courses/387362/lectures/6614531.

DAY 4: WORD OF TRUTH

1. See Isaiah 61:1.
2. See 1 John 4:18.

DAY 5: YOUR REWARDER

1. "G1567 - Ekzēteō - Strong's Greek Lexicon (KJV)." Blue Letter Bible. Accessed November 1, 2023. https://www.blueletterbible.org/lexicon/g1567/kjv/tr/0-1/.

DAY 6: ENTWINING YOUR HEART

1. See Revelation 12:10.
2. Simmons, Brian. "26." In *The Book of Isaiah: The Vision*, 68–68. United States, MN: BroadStreet Publishing Group, LLC, 2018.

DAY 7: BE ALERT

1. Henderson, Robert. Introduction. In Receiving Healing from the Courts of Heaven, 8–8. Shippensburg, PA: Destiny Image Publishers, Inc., 2018.
2. See Luke 22:31.
3. See Ephesians 5:1.

DAY 8: STEADFAST

1. Merriam-Webster.com Dictionary, s.v. "steadfast," accessed November 9, 2023, https://www.merriam-webster.com/dictionary/steadfast.
2. See John 13:35.
3. See Luke 18.

4. See Matthew 9.
5. See Matthew 15.

DAY 9: PORTAL TO GOD'S POWER

1. See Ephesians 2:6.
2. See Ephesians 1:20–21.
3. See Galatians 4:7.

DAY 10: CULTIVATING THE GARDEN OF FAITH

1. "G570 - apistia - Strong's Greek Lexicon (kjv)." Blue Letter Bible. Accessed 2 Feb, 2024. https://www.blueletterbible.org/lexicon/g570/kjv/tr/0-1/.
2. See John 14:14.
3. See Ephesians 4:18.
4. See Hebrews 3:12.

DAY 12: EYES OF HOPE

1. See Daniel 7:25.

DAY 13: SPIRIT, LEAD ME

1. This devotional day was influenced by a book called *Boundaries for Your Soul* by Alison Cook and Kimberly Miller.
2. See Romans 8:7.

DAY 14: COMFORT THROUGH COMPASSION

1. See Job 13:4.
2. See Matthew 5:14–16.

DAY 15: YOU ARE HIS WITNESS

1. See 2 Peter 1:3.
2. See Ephesians 1:17.
3. "H5715 - ʿēḏûṯ - Strong's Hebrew Lexicon." Blue Letter Bible. Accessed November 1, 2023. https://www.blueletterbible.org/lexicon/h5715/kjv/wlc/0-1/.
4. Sheets, Dutch. "Dutch Sheets Testimony." YouTube video, 34:10, June 29, 2013, https://www.youtube.com/watch?v=kqCo01RVOL8.
5. See Judges 7.

DAY 16: HE IS YOUR ROCK AND YOUR DEFENSE

1. *Vocabulary.com Dictionary*, s.v. "security," accessed September 06, 2023, https://www.vocabulary.com/dictionary/security.
2. See Luke 10.

DAY 17: HE IS YOUR REAR GUARD

1. See 1 Samuel 17.
2. See 2 Chronicles 32.
3. Dexter, Geralyn. "How to Spot Manipulative Behavior." Verywell Health, June 15, 2023. https://www.verywellhealth.com/manipulative-behavior-5214329.
4. See Judges 16.
5. See Genesis 19.
6. "H5027 - Nāḇaṭ - Strong's Hebrew Lexicon." Blue Letter Bible. Accessed September 5, 2023. https://www.blueletterbible.org/lexicon/h5027/kjv/wlc/0-1/.
7. See Philippians 3:13–15, ESV.

DAY 18: HE IS YOUR LOVING FATHER

1. Blandino, Stephen. "Four Dimensions of Jesus' Personal Growth." Stephen Blandino, February 4, 2022. https://stephenblandino.com/2015/03/four-dimensions-of-jesus-personal-growth.html.
2. See Luke 15:11–32.
3. See Matthew 28:20.
4. See Romans 5:8.

DAY 19: YOU ARE A CITIZEN OF HIS KINGDOM

1. See 1 Peter 2:9.
2. See Acts 17:28.
3. See Ephesians 6:12.
4. See Ephesians 1:11 and 2:13.
5. See John 15:5.
6. See John 14:12 and Ephesians 1:3.
7. See Acts 1:8.

DAY 20: YOU ARE A CHILD OF LIGHT

1. See 1 Thessalonians 5:5.

DAY 21: HE IS YOUR GOOD SHEPHERD

1. I am grateful for the book *A Shepherd Looks at Psalm 23* by W. Phillip Keller, which inspired this chapter.
2. See Numbers 16.
3. See Deuteronomy 1–16.
4. See 2 Corinthians 10:4.
5. See 1 Samuel 7.

DAY 22: NEW WINE

1. "H3290 - ya'ăqōḇ - Strong's Hebrew Lexicon (kjv)." Blue Letter Bible. Accessed 3 Feb, 2024. https://www.blueletterbible.org/lexicon/h3290/kjv/wlc/0-1/.
2. "H3478 - yiśrā'ēl - Strong's Hebrew Lexicon (kjv)." Blue Letter Bible. Accessed 3 Feb, 2024. https://www.blueletterbible.org/lexicon/h3478/kjv/wlc/0-1/.
3. See Mark 2:21–22.

DAY 23: LOVE FEAST

1. See Job 1:4–5.
2. See 2 Corinthians 12:9.
3. Harris, Murray J. "3 Things 'Lead Us Not Into Temptation' Might Mean-and Which Fits Best." Word by Word, June 9, 2022. https://www.logos.com/grow/4-things-lead-us-not-into-temptation-might-mean-and-which-fits-best/.
4. See Matthew 15:21–28.
5. See 1 Corinthians 11:26.
6. See 1 Corinthians 11:26.

DAY 24: WITH ALL OF YOUR HEART AND YOUR SOUL

1. See Mark 12:30.
2. See Matthew 15:19.
3. See Exodus 15.
4. See John 15:3.
5. See John 7:38–39.
6. See Psalm 119:103.
7. Speicher, Melanie. "May the Words of God Be Like Honey on Your Tongue." Sidney Daily News, March 1, 2018. https://www.sidneydailynews.-com/2018/03/01/may-the-words-of-god-be-like-honey-on-your-tongue/.
8. See Proverbs 4:23.
9. See Ezekiel 36:26.
10. See Jeremiah 24:7.

11. See Psalm 51:10–12, ESV.

DAY 25: WITH ALL OF YOUR MIND

1. See Genesis 1:26–27.
2. Szegedy-Maszak, Marianne. "Mysteries of the Mind Your Unconscious Is Making Your Everyday Decisions." US News and World Report. Accessed September 10, 2023. http://webhome.auburn.edu/~mitrege/ENGL2210/USNWR-mind.html.
3. See Proverbs 27:17.
4. See John 10:27–28.
5. See 1 Timothy 1:7.
6. See 1 Corinthians 2:16.

DAY 26: WITH ALL OF YOUR STRENGTH

1. "G2479 - ischys - Strong's Greek Lexicon (kjv)." Blue Letter Bible. Accessed 3 Feb, 2024. https://www.blueletterbible.org/lexicon/g2479/kjv/tr/0-1/.
2. "H3966 - mᵊ'ōḏ - Strong's Hebrew Lexicon (kjv)." Blue Letter Bible. Accessed 3 Feb, 2024. https://www.blueletterbible.org/lexicon/h3966/kjv/wlc/0-1/.
3. "H1320 - bāśār - Strong's Hebrew Lexicon (kjv)." Blue Letter Bible. Accessed 3 Feb, 2024. https://www.blueletterbible.org/lexicon/h1320/kjv/wlc/0-1/.
4. See 1 Corinthians 6:19.

DAY 27: LOVE OTHERS

1. See Matthew 6:14–15.
2. See James 2:12–13.
3. See Ephesians 4:29.
4. See Luke 10.

DAY 28: GOD'S CULTIVATED GARDEN AND HOME

1. See Matthew 16:16.
2. See Ephesians 3:8.
3. See Ephesians 3:10.

DAY 29: SHADOWS

1. See Isaiah 25:4–5.
2. See Jonah 4.
3. See Mark 5:25–34.
4. See Malachi 4:2.

5. See Isaiah 30:1–3.
6. See John 14:6.
7. See 1 Corinthians 15:54.
8. Fisher, Sarah E. "Tsel: Shadow of Death; Life in the Shade." Hebrew Word Lessons, February 12, 2021. https://hebrewwordlessons.com/2018/11/18/tsel-shadow-of-death-life-in-the-shade/.
9. See Job 10:18–22.
10. See Psalm 107:10–16.
11. See John 8:12.

DAY 30: LOCKING EYES WITH JESUS

1. See Luke 22:60–61.
2. See John 4:17–18.
3. See Luke 19:1–10.
4. See Mark 5:25–34.
5. See Psalm 17:8.

DAY 31: SACRED SORROW

1. See Genesis 28:12–17.
2. Oxford English Dictionary, s.v. "lament, n., sense 1", July 2023. <https://doi.org/10.1093/OED/7455160331>.
3. See Psalm 56:8.

DAY 32: APPOINTED JOURNEY

1. See Leviticus 23.
2. See Numbers 13:26–33.

DAY 33: PEACE REIGNS

1. The Hebrew alphabet. Accessed February 3, 2024. https://www.hebrew4christians.com/Grammar/Unit_One/Aleph-Bet/aleph-bet.html.
2. "The Power of Shalom or Peace of God." Kingdom Life Ministry, February 16, 2022. https://klifemin.org/2021/05/01/the-power-of-shalom-or-peace-of-god/.

DAY 34: ANOINTED AND REFRESHED

1. See Isaiah 61:1–3.

DAY 35: STRAIGHT PATHS

1. See Psalm 119:105.
2. "H5216 - nîr - Strong's Hebrew Lexicon (esv)." Blue Letter Bible. Accessed 3 Feb, 2024. https://www.blueletterbible.org/lexicon/h5216/esv/wlc/0-1/.
3. See Ephesians 4:16.
4. "H3045 - yāḏaʿ - Strong's Hebrew Lexicon (esv)." Blue Letter Bible. Accessed 3 Feb, 2024. https://www.blueletterbible.org/lexicon/h3045/esv/wlc/0-1/.
5. See John 16:33.
6. See John 9.

DAY 36: PROMOTION

1. See Ecclesiastes 3:1.
2. "G1382 - Dokimē - Strong's Greek Lexicon." Blue Letter Bible. Accessed November 1, 2023. https://www.blueletterbible.org/lexicon/g1382/kjv/tr/0-1/.
3. See 2 Corinthians 4:8.
4. See Genesis 22.
5. Voskamp, Ann. *The Broken Way: A Daring Path to the Abundant Life*. Grand Rapids, MI: Zondervan, 2016.

DAY 37: TRUSTING GOD'S JUSTICE

1. See Micah 6:8.
2. Bolen, PhD Barbara. "The Reflex That Can Make You Faint out of the Blue." Verywell Health, April 30, 2023. https://www.verywellhealth.com/vasovagal-reflex-1945072#citation-5.
3. See Ephesians 2:6.

DAY 38: WHEN GOD ANSWERS FROM A WHIRLWIND

1. See Psalm 46:1–6.
2. See John 16:33.
3. See Matthew 28:20.
4. See Isaiah 40:31.

DAY 39: PERSONAL RELATIONSHIP

1. See John 6:35.

DAY 40: FORGIVENESS BRINGS LIBERTY

1. See Matthew 6:14–15.

DAY 42: DEEPLY ROOTED AND BRACING FOR IMPACT

1. See Jeremiah 1:12.
2. See Job 22:28.

ACKNOWLEDGMENTS

Jesus has my first acknowledgment because, without His loving hand upon my life, I wouldn't be here today. You have saved me time and time again from every trap of the evil one. I am honored that You unlocked this message in my heart to share it with the world. Thank You for being my strength when I didn't think it was possible. Thank You for pruning my heart so I could deliver a pure message that is dripping with grace. You are the reason I write, and I pray this book honors Your name.

Thanks to my husband, Isaac. Your constant help and sacrifice are priceless to me. I'm so grateful for your support and love through thick and thin.

Thank you, Mom and Dad. I am honored to be your daughter, and I hope you recognize the impact you have had on my life and my ability to know and hear God personally, which made this devotional possible.

And many thanks to so many incredible friends and family who all lovingly pushed and prayed for me through writing and publishing this book—thank you from my heart.

Thank you to those who have poured into me over the years—Rob and Becca Ketterling, Emily Pahl, Julie Brabec, Megan Egan. You have all been such catalysts to this devotional. I cannot thank you enough for everything you have done.

Finally, I must acknowledge those who helped me with this writing process—David Sluka, Jeremiah and Teresa Yancy, Patricia King, Brian Simmons, and everyone at Messenger Books. Thank you for believing in me as a writer, teaching me how to carry God's message, and encouraging me to see this devotional all the way through.

RECOMMENDED READING

- *Boundaries for Your Soul* by Alison Cook and Kimberly Miller
- *Decree a Thing and It Will Be Established* by Patricia King
- *God is Good* by Bill Johnson
- *Healing the Orphan Spirit* by Leif Hetland
- *Hiddenness and Manifestation* by Graham Cooke
- *I AM Inheriting the Fullness of God's Names* by John Paul Jackson
- *I Give You Authority* by Charles H. Kraft
- *Josiah's Fire* by Tahni Cullen
- *The Judas Goat* by Perry Stone
- *Into the Deep* by Lauren Gaskill
- *It's Only a Flat Tire in the Rain* by Max Davis
- *Miracles* by Eric Metaxas
- *The Opposite Spirit* by Alex Seeley
- *Profound Good* by Blake Healy
- *Rejection Exposed* by Anthony Hulsebus
- *A Shepherd Looks at Psalm 23* by W. Phillip Keller
- *Visions from Heaven* by Wendy Alec
- *The Wilderness: Where Miracles Are Born* by Brian and Candice Simmons

ABOUT THE AUTHOR

Janell Kremer was born and raised in the Twin Cities, MN, where she lives with her husband, two children, and a high-energy border collie named Toka. She graduated from Mankato State University, where she got her elementary education bachelor's degree, and now uses it to homeschool her children. Janell is a passionate teacher of the Word with a calling to see people encounter God's presence and majesty in the face of destruction and desolation. She has a unique understanding of the times and seasons and loves teaching others about the Hebrew calendar and God's appointed times. You can find more about her and her ministry at www.janellkremer.com.

Made in the USA
Monee, IL
20 July 2024